The December Ship

The December Ship

*A Story of Lt. Col. Arden R. Boellner's
Capture in the Philippines, Imprisonment, and
Death on a World War II Japanese Hellship*

BETTY B. JONES

McFarland & Company, Inc., Publishers
Jefferson, North Carolina, and London

The present work is a reprint of the library bound edition of The December Ship: A Story of Lt. Col. Arden R. Boellner's Capture in the Philippines, Imprisonment, and Death on a World War II Japanese Hellship, *first published in 1992 by McFarland.*

Few stories have touched the heart and soul of patriotism like those of the thousands of heroes who fought against overwhelming odds during the war in the Pacific in its early stages. The attack on Pearl Harbor on December 7, 1941, changed the lives of all.

This story belongs to all of them. To the heroes of that time, the World War II years, whose brave experiences inspired history, these pages are dedicated.

LIBRARY OF CONGRESS CATALOGUING-IN-PUBLICATION DATA

Jones, Betty B.
    The December ship : a story of Lt. Col. Arden R. Boellner's capture in the Philippines, imprisonment, and death on a World War II Japanese Hellship / Betty B. Jones.
       p.   cm.
    Includes bibliographical references and index.

    ISBN 978-0-7864-6777-8
    softcover : 50# alkaline paper

    1. Boellner, Arden R.   2. World War, 1939–1945 — Prisoners and prisons, Japanese.   3. World War, 1939–1945 — Campaigns — Philippines.   4. Prisoners of war — United States — Biography.   5. Prisoners of war — Philippines — Biography.   I. Title.
D805.J3J66   2011
940.54'725209599 — dc20   91-50999

BRITISH LIBRARY CATALOGUING DATA ARE AVAILABLE

Front cover image: the "December Ship," the *Oryoku Maru* (courtesy of the Steamship Historical Society Collection, University of Baltimore Library); background © 2011 istockphoto.com

Manufactured in the United States of America

McFarland & Company, Inc., Publishers
  Box 611, Jefferson, North Carolina 28640
   www.mcfarlandpub.com

Preface

The story began with an inherited shoebox full of crumpled clippings, letters and documents that had not seen the light of day for forty-some years. One curious thing led to another. Time and events began to unravel in astounding order.

Could any of the men who served in the same locales with my father during those war years be found? Would anyone remember him? Did I truly want to know the terrible events of what had really happened to him, details that had always been hushed? The search began. Somewhat slowly, somewhat with a painful reluctance.

I found during the search soldiers who remembered, who cared. Each of them, and there were so many, shared their experiences with me. Some had been close friends of my father. What they have given me, the warmth and comfort of just *knowing*, may these pages repay in part.

Betty Arden Boellner

Scottsdale, Arizona

Contents

List of Illustrations

Acknowledgments

My special thanks to:

The American Ex-Prisoners of War Organization
The Fifth Air Base Group Association
The American Defenders of Bataan and Corregidor
The 31st Infantry Regiment Association, Inc.
Walt Regehr
Russell Hutchison
E. Bartlett Kerr
Roy L. Bodine
Betty Rogers Bryant
Morris Shoss
James E. Brown
Albert Gertel
Asbury Nix
The Hon. John McCain
(U.S. Senator from Arizona)
General John McGee
General Paul D. Phillips
Wayne E. Lewis
Jay Pardue
Larry L. Pangan
William Fravel
Carl Nordin
Clyde Hicks
Jack Heinzel
Walter Donaldson
Glenn Nordin
Lloyd E. Mills
Art Bressi
Madeline Ullom

Introduction

Back in New Mexico the trees along the Hondo Valley would be turning. Apples would be getting ripe on Peter Hurd's ranch at San Patricio. And he'd meant to ride that new polo pony Peter had been bragging about, but there just hadn't been time. There would be time when this little jaunt to the Philippines was over. When this "Defensive Precautions" job the United States Army had given him to do was finished. When the Filipino troops were trained and ready. The Japanese would never tackle a sleeping giant like old Uncle Sam. No, never.

It was a fine day for sailing when the elegant *President Pierce* — turned troopship and rechristened the *Hugh L. Scott* — sailed under the Golden Gate bridge on October 27, 1941. Major Arden R. Boellner (pronounced *Bell-nor*), a prosperous businessman from Roswell, New Mexico, stood at the railing with his brother officers. Boellner, an officer in the Army Reserve Corps, was leaving behind his wife, Hazel, and his two daughters, Jeannie, 16, and Betty, 6. He had asked his father to keep an eye on their jewelry store while he was away on a six-month tour of duty.

He quickly made friends with Captain Bill Rogers, another westerner, from Del Rio, Texas. The *Scott* made 400 knots a day, the meals were great, especially the pastries. Boellner was assigned as Field Officer of the Day and inspected every nook of the ship.

They docked in Honolulu on November 2, 1941, alongside a big Japanese ship and a British gunboat. Honolulu was as beautiful as the postcards. He took a tour over the islands to see the pineapple and sugar plantations. This was something to write home about! The *Scott* left Honolulu on November 5, bound for Manila, this time in convoy with another troopship, the *Coolidge*, and a light cruiser.* There was a blackout each night and they heard some news of Japanese activity in

---

*This escort ship was referred to as the Lexington in a November 9, 1941, letter from Major Boellner, and as the Louisville in a November 15 letter.

the Pacific. Still, there wasn't much to do except watch the sea, and eat
fine meals, announced by a Filipino carrying a chime called the "Dressing Bell." Boellner concerned himself with his missing wardrobe trunk.
Maybe it got aboard the convoy ship the *Coolidge*. He hoped so.

They passed Samar on November 19. On November 22, from the
Philippine Department Hostess House, he wrote home. "I'm at Fort
McKinley waiting for my assignment. It's pretty here, but hot and
sticky. I'm worried about Christmas. We hear monkeys at night. . . .
I love all this bamboo furniture. . . . We went by the Walled City, rode
in a calesa. . . . It's Thanksgiving Day. I stored my wool suits at "Joe
Bush Cleaners" in Manila. . . . We don't hear anything about the War
Threat over here." He received his orders a week later. "We sail for
Cebu in 2 hours. I am assigned to the Visayan-Mindanao Force. We
are really some 'punkins over here."

December 7, 1941. Boellner's home in Roswell is filled with concerned friends there to support the family. War is declared against
Japan the next day. He manages to get a radiogram through to them
on December 11. He is all right.

December 26 at Catarman, Samar. "Christmas didn't seem like
Christmas at all," he wrote. The officers sang "Jingle Bells," and had
dinner with an American planter and his family. They hear the politicians are talking in Washington. "Well, let the soldiers do the talking,
and the politicians do some soldiering for a while." January 6, letters
censored. "We're isolated, but I'm okay. There are gold mines here
and the mining companies are helping the army. . . . Took a trip down
the Agusan River. I'm told I am the first army officer ever seen by the
natives." January 28, the first enemy planes are spotted, four of them.
No mail from home. Easter Sunday, April 5, "I'm in a part of the country that looks like the Old West. I'm fine, just homesick." April 12,
Japanese planes and some U.S. The Japanese dropped four "eggs."
"Glad I'm not where I was a few days ago." April 17, "Get Santa Fe
passes for yourselves. Meet me in San Francisco or New York, I'll let
you know where. We're waiting for assistance to get us out. . . . Keep
on being good soldiers."

May 2, 1942. Six Japanese transports and two cruisers were
sighted entering Macajalar Bay, the Cagayan Defense Sector on Mindanao. Regiments were alerted, demolitions placed. The 93rd Infantry took defensive position at Puntian on the loop of the Sayre Highway. The Japanese continued to advance large forces down the Sayre
Highway. By May 9, the Filipino units were scattered and in retreat.
The units were ordered to Sumilao and the 93rd was told it might be

put on its own. On May 10, they were informed of the surrender order for Mindanao. Colonel Dalton, accompanied by his officers, made contact with the commander of the Japanese forces, at which time the American troops surrendered. What had started out to be a brief tour of duty was to become years of starvation and imprisonment.

Boellner, along with the other officers and troops of the Fifth Air Base Group, were imprisoned at Malaybalay, until October 1942, when he was moved, to Davao Penal Colony, where he would remain, together with 2,500 other American POWs for a year and a half. They made the best of things. Japanese Military Prison Camp 2 wasn't too bad—until the escape of ten POWs. But food supplies got shorter. There was no mail from home. When the tide of war began to swing in favor of the Allies, beatings of the POWs increased and the rations grew shorter still. On June 5, 1944, Davao Penal Colony was closed. The POWs were shipped north to Manila.

Boellner spent a few months at Cabanatuan, north of Manila, then was trucked back to Old Bilibid prison in October 1944 to await shipment to Japan.

He boarded the *Oryoku Maru* on December 13, 1944, along with 1,035 other officers, 500 enlisted men, 37 British soldiers, and 47 civilians. It was to be his last voyage. Of the 1,619 sick and starving POWs who endured the torture and bombings while imprisoned in the hold of the ship, fewer than 300 would live to be liberated.

WAR DEPARTMENT
The Adjutant General's Office
Washington

A.G. 210.31 (8-15-41) OA

October 1, 1941.

Subject: Orders.

To: Commanding Officer,
        Fort Huachuca,
        Arizona.

1. Each of the following-named officers of the Infantry is relieved from his present assignment and duty indicated after his name at Fort Huachuca, Arizona, effective at such time as will enable him to comply with this order. He will proceed to San Francisco, California and sail via United States Army transport or commercial liner scheduled to leave that port on or about October 18, 1941 for the Philippine Department and, upon arrival, will report to the commanding general for assignment to duty.

    Major Arden R. Boellner (O-134040), 25th Infantry.
    Major Angus J. Werrell (O-201549), 25th Infantry.
    Captain Roy E. Doran, (O-301611), 25th Infantry.
    Captain Rufus H. Rogers (O-231742), 368th Infantry.

2. The travel directed is necessary in the military service. FD 1408 P 1-06, 15-06 A 0410-2. If the travel from Fort Huachuca, Arizona to San Francisco, California is performed by privately owned automobile, detached service for four days is authorized.

3. The officers named in paragraph 1 should apply to The Quartermaster General, Washington, D. C., for transportation on the October 18, 1941 transport to the Philippine Department.

    By order of the Secretary of War:

Certified a true copy,

T. J. Brogan,
1st Lt FA

-s- J. F. Ruth,
     Adjutant General.

75 CO 25th Inf
25 CO 368th Inf
30 File

-I M M E D I A T E A C T I O N-

Orders from the War Department for Arden Boellner, October 1941.

Letters Home:
October–December 1941

October 1941
San Francisco, California

Hotel St. Francis

Howdy darlings:

Well, I arrived here in good shape. Spent the morning with the kinfolks. Saw both their houses and dogs, and their new plane. We had breakfast at the new Union Station in Los Angeles.

I came in here on the "Daylight," about nine-thirty last night. I have a nice room. I went out to Fort Mason and met Captain Bill Rogers. We were all given yellow-fever and typhoid shots.

We'll be getting on the ship tomorrow. I have stateroom #118. This is all real new to me, but I'm starting to feel like a world traveler already.

You all will have to be the real soldiers in our family until I get back to look after you. Each one of you will have to do your duty, and I'll try to do mine, so you will be proud of me, and grateful to this country which enables us to live and enjoy life. I guess we all have an important part in it after all. If everyone would do as we have to, it would be an even better place.

The waiters are having a strike. There are pickets outside the hotel entrance. I wonder if "Ma Perkins" will let Harry Bridges (the C.I.O. spokesman) go with us out of the country.

Take care of yourselves and each other. Your Daddy is proud of you.

October 28, 1941
Aboard the *Hugh L. Scott*

My darlings:

1

Arden Boellner aboard the *Hugh L. Scott* en route to Honolulu, October 30, 1941.

I'm starting this letter today which I'll mail by Clipper when we get to Honolulu.

The ship I'm on is the *Scott*, which was the *President Pierce* of the Dollar Line. She's 12, 490 tons, built in 1921. It's a hotel with narrow hallways.

We left the dock around two in the afternoon, fooled around in the Bay with practice lowering of lifeboats and using life preservers. Around 4 P.M. we started toward the Golden Gate Bridge. It gave me a strange feeling to be pulling away from land. We began to feel the swell of the sea. We stopped to let the pilot off, and are now making about 12 knots an hour. The ship sways mostly from front to rear. They say the sea is medium today.

I have a stateroom with Captain McKennihan. He's a Mason, too. The room is really fixed up nice with bath and shower. Everything seems to be in miniature, but we are really traveling first class.

They tell me the *President Pierce* made a run to Rangoon before it picked us up to take a bunch of fliers, the American Volunteer Group over there, to fly the "Hump" into China. One of the stewards said they were sure a high-flying, fun-loving bunch while they were aboard. I'd like to have met them.

My trunk didn't make the voyage with me. The quartermaster didn't get it to San Francisco in time. He said it would be on the ship sailing out on Saturday. We're going to wait in Honolulu for this ship, the *Coolidge*, so that will give us about six days over there.

I haven't had seasickness, but there are a number who have. The motion of the ship is like being on a train only the sways are longer.

There are about 500 soldiers from a tank battalion on board, along with two Army nurses and about 50 officers, from lieutenants to colonels. All today.

Wednesday, October 29, 1941
At Sea

I'm better last night and today. Maybe the seasickness pills Dr. Williams gave me had something to do with it.

The scoreboard today says that we made 440 knots in the past 24 hours. The ship is pretty swell, all the lobbies and stairways and lounges are really fixed up. I haven't been to the engine room yet, but I'll arrange that before long.

I got the telegram from Jim McGhee and Allan Falby saying that they were going to send my bedroll and saddle to me collect by Clipper plane.

The sea is a lot smoother today. There are only swells instead of white caps. We haven't seen one ship, or anything else.

From the way it looks now, they won't need rain in this country for a long, long time.

October 30, 1941
Aboard the *Scott*

The sun shines in the morning, so thought I would get some pictures, but this roommate and another officer insist that I play pinochle with them. That takes a lot of time, but it passes the time. That helps.

They found they had two dogs as stowaways. The soldiers smuggled them aboard. I haven't seen them but hear they are just average dogs. They get to go with us all the way to Manila, though.

I'm slated for Field Officer of the Day. Rumor has it we'll be in Honolulu Saturday evening, so I'll probably have to stay on the ship that night.

I dread the drag from there on to Manila. I'm feeling fine, and enjoying the trip. The tank battalion has 54 light tanks on ship-board. I haven't seen them but will as Field Officer.

I hear that we are to have a naval escort on from Honolulu when we join up with the *Coolidge*. I hope my wardrobe trunk is on that ship. If I spot it, maybe I can get the sailors to toss it aboard this one.

Betty — I've been watching the ocean for flying fish. I haven't seen any yet, but will report to you what I see in the way of fish or other ferocious reptiles. They have a picture show each night, which you would like. I get up at 7 A.M. and go to bed sometime from 8 until 10 P.M.

All for Thursday.

October 31, 1941
At Sea

Friday — I made an inspection today for my duties as Field

Opposite: The *President Pierce* [as the troopship *Hugh L. Scott*] was built in 1921. (Courtesy of the Steamship Historical Society Collection, University of Baltimore Library.)

Officer of the Day. I had a chance to get all over the ship except
the bridge and engine room.

Today we saw some flying fish, first I've ever seen. They're
about ten inches long and flutter along with us for about 150 yards,
then go back into the sea. We also saw a freighter about two miles
on our right side. It was going back to the States at slow speed.

We had a fire and boat drill again today about 3 P.M.
Everyone puts on a life preserver which is kept under the bed, then
they go out by their boat number on deck.

We hope now that we will be in Honolulu by Sunday. I'm going to take one of the tours there.

The sunset tonight from the boat was beautiful, and the moon
was shining brightly from the other side of the boat. I'm going to
try tomorrow night to take that with the movie camera.

I'm getting acquainted with some more of the officers. They
all seem like a fine bunch of fellows. Captain Rogers is here in the
cabin with me at this time, and he is looking at magazines. I think
we will go to the picture show after awhile.

We're averaging 400 miles a day. We set our watches back 30
minutes each night. Figuring that way, at home right now it is
about 9:45 P.M. and here it is 6:45 P.M. I guess that is the way we
will lose one complete day.

November 1, 1941
Aboard the *Hugh L. Scott*

Today is Saturday. I had to take this letter out, as I'm writing
to get the finance officer from Tuscon, Arizona, to send me some
of the papers I will have to have over here to get my pay started
again. I have enough there in the bank to keep the present ar-
rangements going along until I get it straight, but please watch the
account until I'm sure my check is coming into it all right. If you
have to have some extra money you can draw on the savings
account.

I am still sailing along fine. At noon we were 266 miles from
Honolulu. We should sight land in the morning. I'm going on a
tour with some of the officers here, they call it a sightseeing trip.

Saw another ship today, and more flying fish this morning.
The weather is getting a lot warmer. I'm sure it is getting cold
there at home, and deer season starts today.

We get some of the news over the radio, and the situation over on the other side doesn't look so good now. But I don't think the sinking of this destroyer will start this thing off yet, and cause us to draw our Navy further back.

We're supposed to have a practice "blackout" tonight. I'm still the Field Officer so have to see what's going on. I'm the second ranking officer on the ship today regardless of all the eagles. Mainly, I inspect the ship all over. I've been everywhere on it now, even the kitchen and the troop quarters.

November 2, 1941
At Sea

Today is Sunday. About sun up this morning I saw the first land in some days. I took a good look at it, too. It was one of the island group. I took a short movie of the sun just showing over the ridge. By seven o'clock we were in sight of the main island. I took more pictures after a man overboard boat drill. We docked about 9:30 A.M.

It is pretty. I saw the big hotels from the ocean. I think everyone is glad for this break in the trip. I'm glad it is now instead of on the way back. For when I start back to the States, they can pass up every place as far as I'm concerned.

There was a big Jap ship in dock here on our way, and an English gun boat of some kind. I took movies of them. The English all wear shorts aboard ship. Kind of nifty, say what?

It is pretty warm. Our cabins are hot at night, but we have fans. I may just stay out on the beach. It's called Waikiki, and looks nice from the sea.

I hope all you folks are fine as I am. There is a lot going on all the time, some kind of entertainment on deck. And it seems we are always eating. We just finish one meal and it's time to eat another. The food is cooked very fine. The pastry is exceptional. It would all be perfect if you were with me. I hope it will be possible someday for all of us to have a boat trip together.

The officers aboard all seem like right fellows. I visit quite a bit with Captain Rogers. He is doing fine, too. I guess us old boys from the west are pretty tough after all.

You all be sweet girls, and love your seafaring Daddy a lot, for now I am a seasoned seaman. But I'm still from the banks of the Pecos River, and I'm still completely sold on that old dry land. I've seen enough water to last me a long time. I'm glad you got home safe and sound from Arizona. I think the highways are the most dangerous thing we have to contend with in this age.

After lunch I'm going to get out and see the city sights. I'll close this letter with the hope that it has a happy sailing by Clipper back to you all. I wish I was a little sheet of paper going along. My love is there. I wonder how long it takes this letter to reach you, for I don't think the Clippers fly every day.

Love, Arden

November 4, 1941
Honolulu, Hawaii

To Dr. L. B. Boellner

Dear Dad:

I took a tour over the island yesterday, and sure did wish you could see it. It's the biggest garden I ever saw. The foliage is beautiful, everything with big leaves and unusual fruits. The only thing I recognized was a prickly pear cactus. I saw bananas, pineapple and sugar growing yesterday. They never have a frost here. None of the houses have chimneys. I took a picture of a water buffalo being worked in about a foot of mud by a native. Also a picture of a native cutting sugar cane.

There are a number of large plantations, both pineapple and sugar cane. There is another kind of fruit, called papaya. They remind you of flat cantaloupes.

We saw the war ships in Pearl Harbor. I guess there were about 12 there. It is a big place. The tour cost $1.50, but was worth $10 to me. We traveled about 169 miles with something to see every minute. This is truly the crossroads of the Pacific. There are all kinds of people here. But everyone speaks English or can understand it.

The prettiest flower I have seen is the hibiscus. They are in many colors, yellow, red, pink. There are some wonderful houses and estates with large fine-kept lawns. I believe the finest we saw was the Mormon temple here.

It's pretty warm since we docked. We have most of our meals

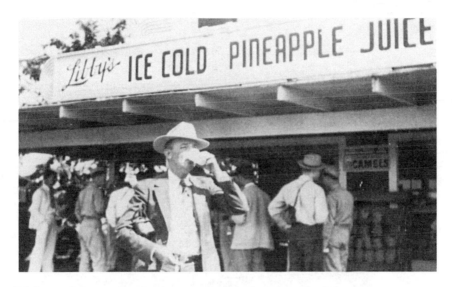

Major Arden Boellner in Honolulu, November 3, 1941. "Drinking pineapple juice. This filling station is located in middle of a pineapple field. It is served ice cold."

on ship. They are really finer than we can get in town for a dollar and a half. Things seem awfully high to me here. Everything is made in the States. The jewelers and opticians have the same lines as we have in the store. In fact, it hardly seems that we are out of the United States proper. The foreign parts of Honolulu are different, of course. There is a Japanese section that I saw from the sightseeing bus.

We will sail again in about three or four days, nothing definite. I met an old friend of mine last night as I was coming back to the boat, Lt. Colonel Herman. I knew him in Nogales, Arizona, in about 1928. He invited me and another officer out to his house for dinner tonight. I'm looking forward to that with interest.

We visited historical places on the island where kings used to hold court and fought some of their battles. There sure are a lot of soldiers and sailors everywhere. I'm getting in all the sights I can, because I don't know when I'll be back to Hawaii. Spotted a Piggly Wiggly store, Kress and Safeway, and A & P. Just the same as at home.

For Betty: This part of the letter is for you. I bet you'll soon be able to read my letters without help. It's always summer here.

In Hawaii, November 2, 1941. Arden Boellner's photo and caption: "The major picking pineapples. There were thousands of acres around this area."

We don't wear coats. There are so many pretty flowers and trees. There are big water buffalos that work in the mud. I bet you'd love to play in *that* mud.

I asked, and there are no poisonous snakes in Hawaii. I don't know why that is, but the people living here are very proud of that fact.

This is a big boat. When I get home I'll tell you all about everything, but it seems to me we are always eating.

I hope you gave your sister a good whoppin' on her birthday.

Seeing one of these little Hawaiian kids would sure tickle you. They are bright and happy kids. Always running and playing and they wear real flowers around their necks, or in their hair.

We'll be sailing again in a few days. I'm glad we got to stop here so I could see a place I've been hearing about all my life.

Be a sweet girl and love your Daddy.

November 5, 1941
Honolulu

Dearest ones:

Just about when we were ready to leave today, we hear that we won't sail until tomorrow. That fits into the picture of Army ways pretty well. I'll probably stay on board until we do.

Yesterday I sent a little package to you all. I started the first movie films back to you, too.

We had a fine dinner and enjoyed the visit with Colonel and Mrs. Herman. They live at Hickam Field, and have real nice quarters. But they sure do want to get back to the States. They know a lot of people from home, so we had quite a visit about home folks. They have two children, a boy who's 15 and a girl who's 14. They have to go to private schools here, and it isn't so convenient for them.

We have just been told that we will sail today after all, at about 4 P.M. I'm going to take this letter to town before we sail. I bought a new pair of white shoes. Never had white shoes before. Maybe someday my trunk will show up.

I expect it's turning pretty cool there. It seems hard to realize. It's hot like the middle of summer here. I'll bet if it wasn't for this ocean breeze this place would really heat up.

I hope things are going along fine there. My interest is there with you all the time. But I'm beginning to realize that the United States Government is really giving me a trip that would be impossible any other way. I'm going to try to take full advantage of it, too.

Love to you all, Your Daddy, Arden

November 9, 1941
At Sea

Howdy darlings:

I may have a chance to mail this by Clipper from the island of Guam. We'll be there in three days. Tomorrow will be Monday instead of Tuesday. We are crossing the date line this afternoon. The sea has been rougher since leaving Honolulu, and the wind has been at our back all the time. The cabins are hotter and we can tell we are really in the tropics.

We are sailing right beside the *President Coolidge*, which has been with us since leaving Honolulu. We also have a Navy light cruiser as an escort vessel, so the three of us are going along together. It feels better to have company.

I'm sure getting anxious to have a letter from you all. There isn't much to do on a ship, and it gets tiresome. Now they have a policy of "blackout" on ship every night. But it's okay. There wasn't that much to do anyway.

I was aboard the *Coolidge* when it docked in Honolulu. It is a little fancier than our boat. It has pretty brass railings and winding stairways. It's about the same size as ours, but they say it rolls worse than our ship. Its passengers were only ashore four hours in Honolulu, and didn't have a chance to see very much.

The hula skirts I sent for the daughters only come in one size. You're supposed to wrap them around your waist somehow to make them fit. Smell like brooms, don't they? I bet you liked the leis — hope they weren't wilted too bad.

I'm worried whether the Army made a deposit for me there the first of the month. I think there will be enough in my checking account to tide over until I get paid, and get the money there to you. I should have drawn every cent coming to me down at Ft. Huachuca, but we would have had to go to Tucson to do it. Since I don't have it, I sure can't spend it. I guess it would be the same as if I was doing it by allotment instead of the way we planned. But it will turn out fine, eventually.

November 11, 1941
At Sea

They had an eleven o'clock ceremony on deck yesterday, short

Opposite: **The luxury liner** *President Coolidge,* **turned troopship (built in 1931). (Courtesy of the Steamship Historical Society Collection, University of Baltimore Library.)**

a more of these menu day by a...

CLOCKS WILL BE RETARDED 30 MINUTES TONITE

Quartermaster Corps
U. S. A.

Thursday   Oct. 30, 1941

U. S.

Transport   " HUGH L. SCOTT "

GPO 3—8230

MENU
d i n n e r
Celery en Branche

Sour Pickles   Green Olives

Radishes

Puree of Navy Beans Soup

Baked Rock Cod   Lemon Butter Sauce
Spaghetti Italienne
Roast Prime Ribs of Beef au Jus
Fricassee Chicken with Rice

Mashed Potatoes   Corn on the Cob
Carrots and Peas

Alligator Pear Salad   French Dressing

Ice Cream
Cakes
Rice Custard Pudding   Vanilla Sauce

Cheese:
American   Cream Brick
Swiss

Saltine Crackers   Fresh Fruits

Coffee   Tea   Cocoa

Menu from troopship *Scott*, October 30, 1941.

we still eat good – Ha – I haven't missed a meal since Sailing –

Q. M. C. FORM NO. 150 (OLD NO. 111)
APPROVED JAN. 23, 1915

Quartermaster Corps
U. S. A.

Monday   Nov 3, 1941

Q. S.

Transport   " HUGH L. SCOTT "

MENU
b r e a k f a s t

Oranges   Grapefruit   Bananas
Stewed Apricots   Preserved Prunes

Bran Flakes   Shredded Wheat   Corn Flakes
Puffed Rice   Grapenuts   Rice Flakes

Boiled Rice with Cream

Fried Pork Sausage
Grilled Breakfast Bacon

Eggs to Order:

Boiled   Fried
Scrambled   Poached

Plain or Chipped Beef Omelette

Saute Potatoes

Hot Buck-Wheat Cakes with Maple Syrup or Honey

Hot Rolls   Coffee Cakes   Dry Toast

Assorted Preserves   Strawberry Jelly
Apple Butter   Marmalade

Coffee   Tea   Cocoa
Ovaltine   Klim Milk   Postum

Menu from troopship *Scott*, November 3, 1941.

Lt. Colonel Rufus H. (Bill) Rogers, 368th Infantry, from Del Rio, Texas.

but impressive. It was Tuesday, but it was Monday. A fellow could get confused this way.

Sometime during the night we passed close to Wake Island. I didn't see it, or know when we passed, but some of the officers saw it. There are some Marines stationed there. And a Pan American Clipper base with its own dock and hotel. Some civilian engineers went to Wake to work on roads and an airfield, so they tell me.

We are making about 415 miles a day. We don't stop for gas at filling stations either. It is hot here in the South Seas. I know what they mean about the tropics. It's a different kind of heat, a wet heat.

It rained for the first time since leaving San Francisco. We didn't need any rain as I can see. The only other place I've been where there is this much water was in Louisiana, when I was on maneuvers there.

I'm guessing it's about 10 o'clock at night on a Tuesday there in Roswell. Here it is 10 o'clock in the morning on Wednesday. I have been feeling fine. We have breakfast at 7:30 A.M., dinner at 12 noon, and supper at 5 P.M. I am in the first dinner sitting. It's announced by a chime carried around by a Filipino boy. They ring the chime a half hour before breakfast, and a half hour before supper. They call it the "Dressing Bell." The meals are fine. I'm eating a lot.

I don't think I ever appreciated my ability as a sailor until I had to do it. This is, I'm told, one of the longest sea voyages that can be made at Uncle Sam's expense. In fact, Europe would make up about the same distance as we were at Honolulu, and that doesn't even include going to Manila.

Captain Rogers is also doing fine, and I believe he is enjoying this trip. I see him a number of times each day. I like him very much.

I'll close for this day, and save some space for the next few days. We think now we will be in Guam about Saturday. I go on as Field Officer again that day, and have to make an inspection of the ship. I have an Officer of the Day, and an Officer of the Guard serving under me to do the usual duties. All I have to do is oversee them.

November 15, 1941
At Sea on Saturday

Today is about 8:30 P.M. Friday there in Roswell. This morning we had a pretty heavy rain. We expect to be in Guam pretty early in the morning. They have warned us against taking any pictures, or even getting out our cameras. I'll have a good look at the place with field glasses.

We are getting pretty well across the Pacific now. It sure does seem like summer to us. I know it's getting cool there at home.

I've made up my mind to one thing. That is, that you kids might not like this trip so well. It gets so tiresome after a few days on the boat. There isn't anything to do but sit around and eat, and sleep too much. Lois Jean might like this life, but Betty wouldn't because there isn't enough room for her to do a good job of running. You might like the six-day trip to Honolulu. But this leg of the voyage, I don't think you'd like it.

Everyone on the boat has about had enough. We have nearly a week more to do. Rumor has it we will be in Manila next Friday. But that can be wrong, like most rumors. It wouldn't be so bad if they didn't have a blackout every night and let the portholes down. It's so hot you can't stay in the cabins. We roam around until about 8 o'clock at night, then try to get some sleep. I wake up at daylight, and get out on deck where it's cooler.

We dress for dinner in the Officer's Lounge each night. We wear a coat, uniform, and tie. I think this is good for the officers to do. We had a little talk by one of the colonels. He said that one of the things all officers had to do was to keep *control* in the Orient by dressing and acting the part of a gentleman at all time. He said that was one of the ways the English have been able to do as much as they have in controlling the natives.

This is really some place for a country boy like me to be. We are going along beside the *President Coolidge* and the cruiser. The three ships stay about a mile apart most of the time. We had some excitement yesterday morning when our ship suddenly began flying the "Out of Control" signal, which was caused by a fuel pump being out of order. One of the other ships closed in for a tow. They had it fixed in about an hour. I told some of the fellows on board that I knew I had made a big mistake when I gave you the Texaco credit card. We could have gotten home with that one.

Betty — I haven't seen any sharks, only little flying fish. No whales either, but I'll keep watching. Some of the time, the ocean looks like laundry blueing water. The old ship cuts right through it and makes a spray of white foam. I'll have some new safari stories for you when I get home. It's too hot here for a good safari. It is real dark at night.

There is a little Filipino girl aboard with her mother. They got on in Honolulu. I think her Daddy must be one of the sailors or member of the ship's crew. She is having a time. She is about four. She puts on her life preserver, just like the rest of us big folks when we have a boat drill. She looks like a little Mexican girl, but she speaks good English.

I guess I am about the fifth ranking officer aboard. I hear there are a lot of lieutenant colonels on the *Coolidge*.

This thin paper I'm typing on doesn't look so good using both sides. But they say only two sheets of this paper in an envelope will go for the usual Clipper postage. The postage from Guam is 40 cents for half an ounce. If they arrive there with postage due for some reason, just charge it up to me.

I hope when I get to Manila there will be some letters from you. Out here on this big blue ocean it sure gets lonesome. You know you are out of contact except in emergency. Being a long way from home is a funny feeling. Something I have never experienced before.

I wrote a letter to Harry Keith (Langford's brother) telling him I was coming to Manila. He's a lieutenant commander in the Navy, and I haven't seen him in about 23 years. I hope I'll be stationed there in Manila. It may be that we won't be so busy over here, and it will be more of a "Gentleman's Job," than was possible in the States. Since about October 6 I haven't done very much to earn my pay. I think I'm just collecting mileage. That pay will help the jackpot some.

I'm worried about this Christmas business. You'll have to have Santa without me this year

It sure will feel good to get my feet on solid ground again. Real solid ground. I just looked out the porthole, and it's raining again. Well anyway — it will settle the dust.

About the strangest thing to me is how long you can wear clothes before they get dirty. I haven't had any laundry done, except a few things rinsed out. I have worn two colored and two white shirts. All my supply of clean clothes is left untouched. I wore my wool uniform as Field Officer, but it was too hot. So I switched to cotton. I'm wondering now how I will ever get everything back in this locker when we leave the ship. Wish I had my trunk.

I still don't know if my wardrobe trunk made connections with the *Coolidge*. I have my white Palm Beach suit and other cottons in it. I'll sure need them when I get to Manila. Maybe it will be there on deck when they unload.

I'm feeling fine. I just need exercise. I walk around for hours at a time, but it isn't enough. I'm sure glad Barney let me buy this typewriter from him. It sure is handy. Some of the other officers have them, too.

Captain Rogers is doing fine. We have a lot of fun talking to each other, especially when some of the other officers come around

to listen to our "line of chatter," Western style. We thought
everybody talked that way. My roommate for some reason stays in
the cabin all the time, even when I kidded him about getting
"prison pallor." He's very studious. He was a history teacher before
he went into the Army. He's a dandy fellow, though.

Fifteen minutes before lunch, so I'll close. I'll write a final note
on the backside when we get to Guam.

November 16, 1941
Guam, The Pacific

Howdy:

Guam is a very small island. The cruiser put up four planes
this morning to guide us into the place where we'll stop for about
two hours. I'm fine, loving you all lots. I hope you miss me a little
bit. We expect to be in Manila by Friday. That is the day after
Thanksgiving, so save me some turkey. Hope you folks are eating
some now, like only you can cook it.

November 18, 1941
At Sea

I sent you all a Clipper letter from Guam. I did some washing
yesterday. It takes about a day for things to dry out. I *will* have
some laundry when we get to Manila. We will have been sailing
for 21 days if we get there Thursday, plus the four days in
Honolulu, that's 25 days since leaving 'Frisco. That's almost a
month. I'll be glad to get there and see what they want me to do.
We should have our assignments soon after we arrive.

I think the Navy may have censored my last letter. We don't
get much news by radio out here. There is some kind of secrecy
going on. Only priority messages coming in and out. And we are
not allowed to even get our cameras out.

The weather is a lot hotter and more humid. Like Louisiana,
where you perspire all the time. We are all going around in shirt
sleeves, except that we still have to dress for dinner in our coats
each evening. The breeze has been from behind us. That makes
the cabins hotter. It seems so strange to think about it being cold
there at home now. I hear they are going to send a bunch of these

officers aboard to Iceland. I think I'd rather have this detail than a cold one. I don't think this one will be so difficult. And it's only for six months anyway.

I'm wondering if our dog Bounce is doing a good job of getting Jeannie and Betty up every morning, like he was trained to do. He'd tear up those stairs in a flash, and head for their rooms. I swear he was smiling when he came out from rousting them up. He'll sure hear from me when I get back, if he's gotten lazy. He is one smart dog.

We hear a lot of rumors about the Japs, and their activity in the Pacific, but personally, I don't put much in it all. I don't think the Japanese are foolish enough to take a chance with what they have out here in any kind of war. The only reason they flare up is on account of Germany having them divert our attention this way some, instead of being a complete help to Britain by being over there in the Atlantic altogether. It is quite a mess. I think it can fold up in a short time, just like it started in a short time and not over so very much at that. Therefore, it shouldn't take much time to close it all down.

If you can find any canned mangos at the stores there, get some and serve them chilled for dessert. They taste like a very sweet peach. We have them quite a bit and everyone likes them. They say we can get them fresh in the Philippines. The Persian melons taste like cantaloupe, but have a rough skin. The papayas are good, you eat them with lemon juice. I also saw them growing in Honolulu. I'm not going to eat any bird's nest soup or the duck eggs with ducks in them, which are considered a delicacy in the Philippines. In fact, I'm going to be careful what I eat and drink.

November 19, 1941
At Sea

The days are passing fast. This morning we saw far away the first of the Philippine Islands. It was Samar. Tomorrow we should be in Manila. I'll save the other sheet to write you all the details. The only address I know of for me is just in care of the Commanding General, Philippine Department. I expect we will have a day or so to get settled in our new locations. I'll be one that sure will be glad to get off this ship for awhile. It gets old after so long.

This afternoon I'm going to try to stuff all my things back into my locker and grips. If I have papers waiting for me in Manila, the first thing I'm going to do is have some money due me sent back posthaste. I hope there will be some letters from you.

Oh, yes — I forgot to tell you that here on the ship we can buy Lucky Strikes for only 65 cents a carton. Strange thing to me that a ship commissary has them at all.

And the way the clocks strike. I'm just now getting to know what port and starboard mean. The port is on the left side facing the front of the ship. Starboard is on the right. At this moment we can see some more islands on the port side, which really means south of us as we are going west.

West reminds me that I wish I was "Out West" in the U.S. right now. I don't think I'm getting the right kick out of the tropics. But I'm glad for the chance to have seen them. I'll sure have a lot to talk about when I get home.

We haven't had any ice on the ship for about a week. The ice making machine is broken down. The refrigerators are still working okay.

Good morning dears: It's Thursday morning, and we are going into our Manila dock now. Will be there in about an hour. *Well, I'm here!*

November 19, 1941
Manila

I'm at Fort McKinley, in a room with three other Field Officers. I'm going to finish this letter and get it out by Clipper. No mail was waiting here. I haven't had a chance to look around much as yet. This place is about five miles out from where the boat docked. It is quite a sight to see this city of Manila.

November 22, 1941
Fort McKinley, Philippine Islands

I'm still unassigned. I hope to know something definite in a few days.

I have decided to send you a check drawn from the savings account. I'm afraid that it will be too long before my checks begin coming there. I don't want you all to be out of money. So take this check to Fred Blocksom over at the First National and have him deposit this amount to the regular checking account, which was set to provide the usual deposit to your account, in addition to an account available for extra money you may need at any time. I'm enclosing a check for $500 from savings to checking. Also I can cash checks here on this account through the post exchange up to $100, so I think this will solve the problem until they start getting my pay deposited. Then we will put this $500 back into savings.

We don't have our assignments, and the baggage and mail is all mixed up. I haven't had a letter, or even a newspaper from home. I'm not sure what can be done about Christmas shopping, either. Everyone here doesn't seem to realize it takes time to get things back there for Christmas, so I guess, dear ones, the burden of doing most of it will fall on you this year. But please do it nicely, to make up for my not being there, too.

The days are hot and sticky. The nights are cool enough for us to have some cover, believe it or not. I'm feeling fine. It isn't so bad if you forget you are so far from home and all you kids. It sure is lonesome, and you would be surprised how few white people we see in Manila. Out here at the fort, there are only officers. There aren't any officers' families on the island, so no social affairs. We'll probably be here for about another week. I started a radio message to you through FALCONI yesterday. I had to mail it to the amateur operator here. I hope he gets it, and sends it on out to you all. When I get to the city I'll look him up and ask him about it.

I saw Lt. Colonel Killen. He was head of the Tucson office where I used to send my correspondence courses. He just came over with us. I talked to him a little bit. So there have been changes sure enough in this old Army. I see Captain Rogers every day. He is billeted with the other captains in another building.

                    Bye today, my dears

November 22, 1941
Manila

Whoa—there is more. I am sending this out regular mail and sending some stamps that aren't any good over here.

We went to town again today. Tried to see the finance officer but they were so busy they couldn't get my work done. I'm going to eventually get some money in the bank for you all. I'm making an allotment to the bank for $250 a month, so your money will be there for sure.

I looked around for Christmas gifts, but can't find what, or the place I'm looking for yet. I got me by luck an "Elephant Hunter's Hat." They are worn here all the time, and everyone was about sold out. Also some new khaki clothes. I don't know where the wardrobe trunk is as yet.

I'm feeling fine. The nights cool off about 11 P.M. Say, did you know that all the cars here drive on the left side of the road? It is a scary experience riding in a taxi. We go to town for 25¢ our money. They have their own money here, ours is worth twice as much as theirs, but prices on most things figure out about the same. A meal will be two pesos, or $1 our money.

Betty—we hear the monkeys around here at night. But I haven't seen them as yet. Don't know whether I can catch one and send it to you or not.

I think I'll send, or bring back, some bamboo furniture from over here. It looks real nice. We can fix up a room with it. It's especially suitable for a sunroom.

There are the most unusual sights around here. The worst thing is that it is so dirty and sticky. I'm kind of afraid to get where the best sights are. But I'm interested in seeing them.

The natives are all small, the soldiers are small, about 90 lbs. or less. The ponies pulling the rickshaws (I think they are called *calesas*) are small. The *calesas* are two large-wheeled carts all painted up fancy, with lots of shining brass, and big fancy lamps on each side.

I saw them doing the washing in the river where they "spank" the clothes with a paddle or a rock. The old Spanish fort, called here the "Walled City," is very large and extensive. But it looks like a dungeon and is full of Chinese living nearly like rats. There are very few flies here. Many places have no screens at all. I don't know why—for from the smells, there should be flies.

The shutters on this building are made of wood, not glass. They have some kind of shell that lets light through. All the electric light shades are made of shells wired together. Odd, but nice.

I bought a bolo knife yesterday. Only kind of knife I don't have, I guess. If I don't send it on home, I'll bring it back with me.

We don't have our assignments yet. Rumor is they may move me some distance from Manila. I'm about five or six miles southwest of Fort McKinley. This is a big post. We eat at the Officer's Mess, the meals are fair. One thing they don't seem to have here is fresh milk. The milk we use comes in cans from Australia and China.

Everything seems to be made from bamboo, or mahogany, and oh yes, coconuts.

I sent the check out. Have to attend a meeting. Love to all alike.

November 27, 1941
Thanksgiving Day
Fort McKinley, Philippine Islands

My darlings at home:

This is Thanksgiving Day for most of us. This year is somewhat lacking in being able to get into the real spirit of the thing. I am starting this letter and will send it by Clipper when I have my assignment.

We are just going to be here for a little while. We will probably be sent out to one of the Division Camps. We had a talk by one of the generals yesterday, and received some of the first information we have had, in fact the *only* information we have had since arriving. It is essentially this—we are to be *advisors* to the Philippine Army, and our job will be as instructors. He says the officers with each of their regiments have not had a chance to get tactical training. I don't think the job will be hard work, in the amount of work, but from what he said I expect that "Yours Truly" will have a grass house and about five boys running around waving their hands and talking a language that they themselves are sometimes pressed to understand. Very few speak English, and most of them will let you think they understand when they don't.

Fort McKinley looks like any other Army post, except there is grass everywhere and some nice trees, and there are these funny looking *carabao*, or cows with funny looking horns, running around just outside the gate. The natives live in grass houses all around the post. The buildings are very substantial, roughly built from mahogany, then painted a cream color. The roofs are corrugated tin, painted a dirty red color.

The trees are the prettiest they have here with vines running up them with more big leaves. The bushes all have flowers on them, like the ones in Honolulu. Oh, yes — and on our tables every night for most meals there are poinsettias! I haven't seen an orchid yet. If I did, I didn't recognize it. I haven't taken movies yet, but have elaborate plans for some. There have been restrictions about cameras, something to do with "infiltrators," or something like that.

I sent out some Christmas cards, just signed by me. They were addressed to the Mr. and Mrs.'s who are our friends. I wrote some of them a letter with it. I hope they get back there before Christmas. I'll leave the big list for you to do.

Also I sent all you kids and Dad, too, a very similar gift, which I had made up to what I hope were the right measurements. They are supposed to be pretty nice over here, but I don't know.*

I also sent Hazel's birthday gift for January 6. It might arrive before her Christmas gift with the mixed-up mail these days. It all depends on when the ships sail, the route they take, things I have no control over. But I'm trying to do things ahead. At least they get done that way.

I haven't seen hide nor hair of my confounded wardrobe trunk, or the box of books supposed to be sent to me from Ft. Huachuca (Arizona). I had them radiogram to San Francisco yesterday, asking where the devil those things were. My guess now is that transportation over here is one of the most unreliable things they have.

At the port yesterday they told me there were to be five ships in some time next week. The trunk could be on any one of them. Well, I sure hope so. I have stored all my wool suits here with me, believe it or not, with "Joe Bush Cleaners" here in Manila. That's my dark suit, the gray one, my wool uniforms, and cap. When I *do* get the trunk I will do the same, provided that where I am they will have such a service.

I now have two new khaki uniforms and am having two more made, as well as one white duck suit. So with another white suit, if I stay around here long enough, I'll be fixed up. I also have a pair of white duck shorts just like the British wear. They call them "short pants" and they are not considered regular uniform. They'll

---

The gifts from Manila were monogrammed linen lounging sets for each family member.

do for port wear, though. So now I am looking "just ducky." A lot of the other officers are following suit, if you'll excuse a pun.

Our meals at the Officer's Club are not unusual in any respect, except that you can order what you like from those Filipino waiters, and you will probably get what they can get a hold of first. If you order anything extra, about three of them will all bring you the same thing at the same time. They try very hard to please. I sure get a kick out of it all. They aren't sure what you want, and will say "yes" when they mean "no." But they never say "no." They can understand Spanish better sometimes, but not all the time.

In fact, even their own language, which is called "Tagalo" around Manila, is not understood by the natives 25 miles away. They can't talk to each other, and I'm told it's nearly impossible for white folks to learn that language, even experts. The highest class of natives speak English, but they are a minority. The women over here seem to be stronger and healthier looking than the men, who look very small, and sort of shriveled up. Some of them have a sissy manner about them which I can't understand. I'm told they would rather work around a house than get out and do a soldier's job in the field. Maybe that's why so many of them are house boys, and good ones. They do laundry, cook and sew, and want to please. The women are out in the rice fields doing a lot of the hardest work. I'll investigate the system further, and see if it might apply to my household when I get back. (Joke there.)

Betty — a lot of the big girls here are not as big as you are now, and not nearly so pretty.

Last night we had an open air show here, a festival of some kind. It was as good as anything I've seen in years. They had some Australian dancing girls, and natives and Orientals which sure can do the hula. Some do acrobatic dancing, where they put one foot behind their necks and stand on one foot for 10–15 minutes, then change feet and do it all again. They were really graceful, and dance like I've never seen before. One of the girls did most of her dancing with her arms and hands. She was beautiful, and so graceful.

Then they had some fine singing by a native girl. The tumbling team was good, too, so I really got to see a dandy show. It didn't cost any money, being here on the post. There must have been 2,000 people there. The front row was reserved for officers. We were comfortable and could see just fine. The backdrop for the stage was two turkey gobblers facing each other. They were at least 20 feet high, and all painted nice.

We're just marking time around here waiting for our assignments. When I know where I'm going, I'll include that in this letter, and maybe, pretty soon, I can expect to start getting some mail from home. This Clipper business is best, but it's expensive.

I still have a hunch I'll be coming home in April. That's why I'm trying to see all I can in the time I'm here. If they fix me up with a private car, which they say they will do, I can really get around. Even if they send me to some of the Southern Philippine Islands, I'm supposed to have a staff car.

I will probably be a regimental instructor, or regimental commander with one of the ten divisions of the Philippine Army. We are to be the same as designated officers with the National Guard Divisions in the States. We were told we would only be there on temporary duty until we can get them better trained than their officers have been able to do. Then when their own officers can take over again, we will be withdrawn.

I'm guessing we will be with them about six months. That's just a guess. I think it will be most interesting. We don't have a lot of things to contend with like at the regular army posts in the States. I believe most all of the American officers over here are pretty good, and don't have that complex so outstanding in many of the regular Army officers elsewhere. And too, most all of the officers over here didn't want to come, and that makes a difference. So we feel we will do our best to get the job done and *then get out of here*.

We were told that most all of the soldiers in the Philippine Army have had only about five weeks of training, except for the noncommissioned and commissioned officers, who have had a lot more. There will be from five to eight of our own officers with each regiment, and a few American enlisted men who will assist us officers.

We don't hear anything about the "War Threat" over here. They are only preparing this army, and trying to get them trained. I can't find Howden* or his bunch yet. They must have been sent on ahead to some other island. We don't think we'll see much of the American troops over here anyway, but will confine our work to the new Philippine Army.

*Ted Howden was the Episcopalian chaplain from Roswell, New Mexico, who accompanied the New Mexico units to the Philippine Islands in 1941.

The last three days have been some cooler. I don't think this climate will be so bad, especially if I get to go to a camp in the mountains.

November 29, 1941
Fort McKinley

Well, today we received our orders. My orders are #SO-277, Headquarters Philippine Department. It lists 12 lieutenant colonels, three majors, ten captains, nine lieutenants, and we are all ordered to Headquarters, Visayan-Mindanao Force, Cebu City, P.I. This city is located on an island about 300 miles south of here, and is the second largest city on the island, nearly in the center of a group of islands all south of here. They say there are many features of this place that we will like just fine. It's cooler, and doesn't rain so much.

Captain Rogers is going there, too, as well as any number of fellows I know from the boat. That includes the captain I shared the cabin with. I expect we will be comfortable and able to get things arranged. Maybe we will live in a hotel or other suitable quarters. I expect there is some mail here on the island somewhere, but service has sure been bad. I haven't received anything but your Clipper letter. I am glad for that letter. Maybe the mail will catch up with me, along with my wardrobe trunk and books someday.

They sent a radiogram back to San Francisco about my trunk. But I have yet to be told anything as to where it is.

I'm not sure what the new address should be. I think the mail comes here to Manila first. It might be all right to send it to: Major, Infantry, U. S. Army, USAFFE, Cebu City, Cebu, P.I. In fact, try it until you hear a change. Now don't that sound real foreign enough for anyone? Cebu is a city of about 125,000.

December 1, 1941
Manila

We sail for Cebu in two hours. This is a smaller boat, but I sure have a dandy cabin for all my baggage.

Have this check I've enclosed put in the bank for our account. Also, starting January 1, 1942, there should be $250 a month sent

to the bank from Washington. Also, I am opening an account with
the Philippine Trust Company in my name, and your name, subject to your drawing on it by New York draft.

I'm fine. And just this minute your Clipper letter came and
one from Dad and the store bunch. That's sure fine. I'm glad even
if they're late. Tell everyone hello. I'll answer when I can. I'm glad
to get going again.

We are really "some punkins" over here. Be sweet and think
about me "Once in Awhile."

Love to you all, Arden

Roswell, New Mexico: December 7, 1941

The big, woody brown, gabled house was rapidly filling with family friends, dressed in their Sunday best. This was Arden Boellner's home, built by his father, Dr. Louis B. Boellner, in 1910 on wheat field land near the Spring River, in a sturdy New Mexico town named Roswell. It was a cold, bright, sunny day with just enough of the brisk frontier wind for hurrying inside.

"Arden will get back from the Philippines. He'll find a way," Judge James McGhee, Arden's good friend, said as he took a sip from his coffee cup. His Stetson was new. He had forgotten to take it off when he came through the front door.

"We'll beat the devil out of them," Gayle Armstrong, another of Arden's friends, said from his armchair.

"They're putting sandbags around the telephone building in San Francisco. The whole west coast is on alert. Damn — how could this happen? Where's the Navy? Where's the Army? Why didn't somebody spot those Jap planes?" Willis Ford moved into the circle of Arden's hunting buddies. Mrs. Lowe from next door bustled by him carrying her specialty, a chocolate layer cake destined for the kitchen.

The aroma of freshly brewed coffee, the strong ranchman's coffee, drifted from the kitchen. The service door between the dining room and kitchen creaked open and shut in a rush of activity. Women dressed for church put on aprons, washed cups and saucers, sliced cake, baked morning rolls, made tea sandwiches, and talked in hushed tones.

"Someone should go upstairs with Hazel and the girls," said Frank Mulkey (her given name was Frances, but none of her Roswell friends had ever called her that).

"Bess is with her," Thelma Crosby poured orange juice into a dozen little striped glasses. Thelma was at her best in crowds. Her husband, Bob Crosby, had been a World Champion cowboy in 1928. She

31

ASSOCIATED PRESS LEASED WIRE.   SECTION ONE   "TODAY'S NEWS TODAY"   ROSWELL, NEW MEXICO   SUNDAY, DEC. 7, 1941

U. S. AT WAR, JAPS
ATTACK HAWAII AND MANILA AT NIGHT

JAPAN ATTACKS HAWAII AND THE PHILIPPINES

Headlines in *Roswell Morning Dispatch*, December 7, 1941.

Arden Boellner's home on Missouri Street, Roswell, New Mexico.

had dined with Lady Weigall in Westminster Hall only four years before. She loved people, and they loved her.

"Arden was on his way to Manila, wasn't he? Maybe his ship turned back in time."

"I think he was already in Manila. Oh, I just wish we knew something," the ladies moved with precision in the kitchen. They had had a lot of practice over the years.

Elderly little Mrs. Dakens, in her flower pot hat and lace gloves, fussed over the bread crusts she was trimming away.

"The Japanese are such polite people. Why would they do such a thing?"

"Wait—there's another tray to go to the table—and I think that one coffee pot is about empty."

They were all here now, milling from room to room, landmark people of a good town who had come as friends to offer support. Other friends were busy calling the 940 number of the Boellner residence. "Just tell Hazel we're thinking about her—"

The phone rang again. "Any word at all as to where Arden might be?"

"Hang on a minute, I'll let you talk to Bert."

Bert Ballard, Arden's friend from their cadet days at New Mexico Military Institute in Roswell, took the phone. The caller was Pat

EXTRA

ROSWELL MORNING DISPATCH

EXTRA

VOLUME XVII

NUMBER 70

(ASSOCIATED PRESS, KING AND UNITED FEATURES)

ROSWELL, CHAVES COUNTY, NEW MEXICO, THURSDAY, DECEMBER 11, 1941

GERMANY, ITALY DECLARE WAR ON UNITED STATES;

U.S. CONGRESS TO VOTE FOR WAR AT NOON TODAY

McNalley. Pat owned one of the best beauty shops in town. She had a cold, but she was coming over anyway.

"Arden will make it back. We have to believe that," Bert was saying. "MacArthur is over there, too. He'll get it all straightened out. I know that we're Republicans, but that doesn't help us any today." One of the ladies set a sandwich plate down on the phone bench beside him.

"Hazel is bearing up fine. She's upstairs. Betty is playing with her paper dolls, and Jeannie went over to Phyllis' house. Yes — if you want me to, I'll go out in the yard and make sure Dr. Boellner is doing all right. He doesn't like all this confusion and noise. I know he wears a hearing aid. I can't stop the war — try to pull yourself together. We'll all get through this."

George and Muriel Carothers had just driven up in their green Buick. George still walked with a cane from his World War I days in France. It would take him a while to climb the long sidewalk up to the house.

December 7, 1941
Roswell, New Mexico
Letter Returned Undeliverable

Dear Daddy, Please come home. I ate a melted cheese sandwich at the Victory Cafe. Mother and Jeannie are crying. Miss Lea is my teacher.

Love, Betty

Opposite: **Headlines in** *Roswell Morning Dispatch*, **December 11, 1941.**

Letters:
December 1941–April 1942

December 26, 1941
Catarman, Samar
Philippine Islands

My darlings at home, — Howdy!

I'm starting this letter, which is number eight. I'll write along on it every day, so then I'll have a regular letter ready to send when I get a chance to get anywhere to mail it.

Well, yesterday was Christmas. I'll say it was the most unusual Christmas I have ever known. It didn't seem like Christmas at all. Christmas Eve the four of us sang "Jingle Bells," and tried hard to remember the words, "'Twas the night before Christmas when all through the house —" We had some fun acting silly, but the difference in what we used to do on Christmas Eve, and what there was for us to do here — well, it made the situation comical.

Yesterday we got all dressed up in our best uniforms. We were invited for dinner at Mr. Hutton's house. He's an old American who has a native wife. He has been here for about 54 years, so he doesn't have many of the American ways about him anymore. He tried to have some American food for us. It was really fixed up pretty well. I had a bottle of beer before dinner, then some kind of soup with rice in it. Then roast young pig, native-type, no doubt. Also baked chicken with mashed potatoes. The dessert was some kind of pudding.

One of his girls is about seven years old. I gave her my card with Betty's name on it. I told her to write Betty, and that Betty would be glad to hear from her. I think he has three children younger than she is, and one older. One of the boys is blonde and about three years old. They live upstairs over his garage, and seem

36

to be fixed up as well as many of the people here. I guess he made some money out of coconuts. He told me he had a large plantation back in the mountains. Also, his family plans to be back there in a few days until things settle down a little better along the coast.

We took some pictures yesterday. I hope they are good There are some of the Filipino officers who came around to visit for a Christmas present.

I haven't heard from Captain Bill Rogers since I left them on Bohol. I wrote him a note a few days ago. Maybe I'll hear from him pretty soon. I heard a rumor that they sent his outfit on south, but we don't know anything for certain. Even the radio war news doesn't give us anything, as the censors make a prepared statement that is read out. I bet you all at home know more than we do about what is going on.

Oh, yes—I forgot to mention that we celebrated Christmas by going into the ocean again. We swam about an hour. It rained yesterday morning.

Last night the Filipino officers got up a little dance at their quarters. They were able to round up about five or so native girls. I didn't go over, but one of our officers did. He said it was quite some affair for a dance without hardly any girls. I think it was over about nine o'clock.

I'm convinced that the scarcest thing on these islands is white women. I think I saw three or four in Manila. And they were white Russians, someone said. It's a good thing that all the American women were moved out of the islands around here some time back. Now there won't have to be the necessary planning for their protection. I expect the next few weeks will decide about defense plans for these islands. The enemy seems to be making an all-out effort on Luzon now, and if they get dug in there, there's a chance for them throughout the islands.

It seems to us that is what they are after. I hear over the radio that they are talking in Washington—well, I think it's high time to stop all the talking and get busy, and begin doing some things. They haven't been able to talk anyone out of anything, and the more they talk, the more it costs us, one way or another.

Maybe the way to solve it would be for the *soldiers* to do some of the talking for awhile, and let the *politicians* do some real soldiering. I know some I'd love to give orders to.

The mosquitos are pretty bad, but thank goodness, no chiggers. The old chigger scars from Louisiana still show a little.

Arden Boellner's daughters, Lois Jean and Betty, with the family dog, Bounce, January 1942. (Family photo copy.)

    I was just thinking how glad I am to have this typewriter, and I'm grateful to Byron for it.

December 28, 1941
Roswell, New Mexico
Letter Returned Undeliverable

The Boellner family as the new year begins, January 1, 1942. (Courtesy of *The San Angelo Standard Times*, San Angelo, Texas.)

Dear Daddy, I got a Scarlett O'Hara doll with clothes for Christmas. Grandaddy has pecans and a cold. Please come home.

Love, Betty

January 12, 1942
Roswell, New Mexico

Letter Returned Undeliverable

Dear Daddy,
Georgine is my best friend. We eat mayonnaise and crackers after
school. Bounce likes her too. When can you come home?

Love, Betty

January 6, 1942
Somewhere in the Philippines

Resumed this letter today. There have been a few days between letters. I sure have been a busy person. There are a lot of
things happening, especially since our move from the island of
[Samar]. We have hit a lot of rain and have been slowed up a lot
since we arrived here. We hope to be able to get going as soon as
the water goes down below some of the bridges.
Today is Hazel's birthday. So to celebrate I invested in a
radiogram back home. I hope it will make the grade. I'm doing
fine, trying to get some reliable word back to you. The island is a
wet one. They moved the entire outfit [from Samar down to
Leyte]. We made it in good shape, but we all missed a lot of sleep.
I went for four days without taking my clothes off, let alone getting
cleaned up. We expect to move on down to [Mindanao] as soon as
possible, and may have an area which will be somewhat stable for
a while. We are hearing some good news rumored over the radio. I
guess things will improve rapidly. We just don't have any mail
contact with anywhere these days. I'll have to take a chance on getting a letter out to you by air.
I'll bet after all of this is over we'll wonder at all the unusual
things that have been happening. You talk about feeling that you
are isolated from the rest of the world — well Byrd didn't have

*In many of the letters place names or other information deemed important to keep secret for
the war effort were censored. Through research, and in some cases because words were legible
underneath the censor's ink, I have been able to recreate missing text. These insertions appear
in brackets.*

anything on us when he was in Little America! At least he had a dependable radio that didn't have to be sent in code, and he could listen all he wanted to.

This is a very interesting place. There are a lot of white men over here that sure have been giving us assistance, and all we could hope for at this time. There are some of the best gold mines in the world here, but, of course, they are not working them now. These miners are the ones who are being the greatest help to us in anything we want. It has been raining here all the time since we have been here, so you know what we have been doing. Watching it rain.

It was [on short notice] that we received our orders to move in a hurry and had a long trip [to make] by bus and ship, over rough roads and rough seas, which took us about three days. But as far as I know, we made the move entirely unknown to anyone but ourselves, and without serious incident. Except that I was personally scared twice [when bombers flew over us, and a strange ship at sea played hide and seek with us until we slipped away in] a cloud of rain.

By the way I have been informed that I was recommended for promotion to lieutenant colonel. I haven't had anything official on it. That could be because we move faster than a telegram can find us. I don't have a chance to get silver leaves now, so will have to wait.

Well, the radiogram did not get through. I had to get my money back which is quite a job over here. Reminds me of trying to get your money back from one of our post offices.

January 14, 1942
Somewhere in the Philippines

I'll bet you all are wondering where I am, and what is going on over here these days. I'm now at [Butuan]. In the last week I have been as busy as can be. I am now a regimental commander. I have a regiment all of my own and I'm the boss. I have been expecting my promotion to come through every day, but like everything else over here, it takes a long time to get mail. The mail is held up by boat situations, stacked up and awaiting orders and other notifications as to when it will be put on a boat.

We hear a rebroadcast of news once in a while. Today it sure did sound pretty good. However our news is not extensive. It's pretty hard to get the full picture.

There are a lot of mosquitos here, and it is pretty warm, but there is pretty scenery. We are getting along fine. I feel fine and am doing well. I sure would like to have some news from home one of these days.

I hope it won't take us very long over here to get this job done. Now I have a substantial command and a big job in a big country. One of my missions is very interesting. A river problem with small boats.

January 18, 1942
Mindanao, Philippine Islands

It has been a few days between the last of the letter on the other side and this one. Well, I think now that I have been able to get a radiogram through to you all. I was glad that they told me I could get it accomplished via RCA. I have been informed by the adjutant that I was promoted to lieutenant colonel effective January 15, 1942. I'm still without my orders. It may be some time before I get them. I tried to tell you in the radiogram. Guess it got through all right.

We sure are busy over here. It keeps us on the jump all the time to keep things moving. Everything seems to get done some way, but so slowly. That seems to be the Filipino way of doing things. The enemy has not been active around here, except for air observation. But we have to be prepared in case they start anything.

It will be pretty nice when I can tell some of our Army back there how to do a lot of things that we have to do over here the hard way. I'm going to [Lake Mainit] in a day or so to make an inspection. Even if I could tell you the names of some of these places, you all don't have maps there that would help much. So I'll have to wait and show you my maps and explain it all to you. It really is interesting work.

By the way, day before yesterday I spotted some new officers. They turned out to be two officers who came over on the boat from the States with me. We had quite a visit. They were looking around [Butuan] Ha! Censor, I fooled you and didn't say it. It sure did seem good to see them though. I think they felt the same way.

One time while I was in bed I felt an earth tremor. It was kinda like a cinder-shifting motion. Just rolled you around a little bit.

I asked the colonel what he was doing about getting his letters off. He said, "I'm just writing them, and filing them " But we are both watching for a way to get them mailed.

I can see how it takes a long time to get things going over here. The time and power to get things done has to be considered. But I believe things are getting better each day now. It won't be long until we are clear over here. I would like to hear the news as it is now being broadcast over there. Unless they censor yours too. We get some shortwave news from San Francisco over here. We have a general idea of what is going on.

Maybe after all this is over, they plan to send us over to Japan to make sure that they behave. It would be okay for about six weeks. I have had all of it I need over here. There is still so much work I left in the States to do. But if they think I'm needed over here for a while longer, then I guess I'll have to give in and help them out.

January 25, 1942
Mindanao, the Philippines

After some more delays that don't make much difference since there isn't any mail service to the States yet that we know about anyway, it's now Sunday, and I have been busy lately again. I have just completed a trip up the [Agusan River to its source] and what an experience that has been! I'm told *I* was the first United States Army officer ever to be seen up there by the natives!

I made a trip to the [south-interior] jungle of this island. We had .22 rifles with us and other small arms. We saw monkeys, and every kind of parrot, and other kinds of colorful birds native to this land. I was on three kinds of boats, and had very little sleep, and very little food that I could eat, for four and a half days. It was an experience! I wouldn't take anything on earth for it, and probably never will have that chance again.

I had a native jeweler make some silver leaves for me so now I have the lieutenant colonel insignia. I have a regiment, and look for a full colonelcy now. If Judge Jim and the boys there will get busy, maybe I can be a general pretty soon. It takes an Act of Congress to get that job done through some recommendation by senators or the War Department. (Tell them to be sure and spell my name right.)

I think now I was able to get a radiogram through to you all. It hasn't been returned, and we were told in advance that we could. I wanted you all to know I am fine, and doing okay. I sure would like to hear from you all, but I'll have that to look forward to. What letters do come, and there sure are a lot of them gathering up somewhere I guess, will sure be welcome. I took some pictures upriver. I've had some developed. You will sure get a kick out of them. I can't send them to you as yet, but I will when I can.

I haven't seen anything of my wardrobe trunk. The first Jap I see with some of my clothes on, I'm going to give him a run and get them back. I guess the clothes I left in Manila are being divided up among some of the Jap officers. But that will be Willis Ford's worry, for he wrote the insurance for them.

I'm going to send a copy of this letter by regular mail right away and hope it gets through. I'm not sure if the Clipper is running. Maybe the regular mail will pick it up before the Clipper does.

I'm hoping and believing that all of you are getting along fine, and doing just as I hope you are. Tell everyone hello for me. It isn't as bad over here as I'm afraid a lot of you think it is. But I sure will be able to tell you a lot of tales.

Betty, I've got some new safari stories to tell you when we play "Safari" again, because this is really safari country. Some actual experiences are good for a few choice stories.

I've had to quit being so finicky about my eating. I still try to be careful. I don't take chances, but when I was on a small dirty boat I did get my stomach upset. That was during our trip to [Tacloban] about a month ago. There are a lot of things I would sure like to tell you about — what we're doing, and getting done. But that will have to wait until the letters aren't opened by censors.

I think this will not last long. I hope my guess is right this time. I missed my guess about having to go to war with Japan. I imagine you all over in the States are getting serious about this business now. We feel like the pressure will be off over here pretty soon, if we can just get a little help from the Navy and the Air Force. We can look after the ground, but air and water are out of our line a little. So line up some specialists over there, and get

them over here. Then we can have this business in the bag all in
short order.

There is a Mr. and Mrs. Varden over here who are white
folks. They have been nice to me and I sure do appreciate them.
She is the only white woman I know of around anywhere. She isn't
like a lot of them that ran to the hills when the war started. She
stays right here and doesn't even consider getting back into the hills
like most of them have done, including some white men. Near an
army is about the safest place for civilians to be.

This is great gold mining country. Some of the best mines are
scattered around here. The mine officials have been very fine to the
Army. Mr. Varden is superintendent of one of these mines. We
have been able to get a lot of essential equipment and supplies
from these mines, as they are really big outfits.

It is a funny situation. I have already been made at least a
lieutenant colonel, and I haven't even received my official notification. When I do get it, if ever, I will have been made a lieutenant
colonel since the first day of this year. My job responsibilities are
the same as Colonel Davis' at Ft. Huachuca (Arizona), only I have
to operate during the war in the field with my regiment. Anyway,
it will be easy to look after all this business back home in a post.
Especially in peacetime. But they might not want me then, and I
may not want to do it either.

I sure do have some good American officers as my [executive
staff.] I only wish I had a few more like them, but we are [very short
of officers.] I have some real good Filipino officers, too. Two of them
have been through our service schools in the States at Ft. Benning,
Georgia. All of them are from the Filipino West Point on Luzon.

I imagine that General MacArthur will be able to hold better
than his own with the enemy up there on Luzon. And when the
turn comes he will be on top. I imagine he has had it pretty rough
up there because of the surprise element, but I'll bet he will be able
to turn in a good score before it is over. We hear that all American
civilians up there are all right.

I hope that the government made a deposit there for one
month's salary, and that they are keeping it safe for me
somewhere. We don't need much money here, for there isn't
anything to spend it for. With the allotment made back there for
you all, everything should be fine from a financial standpoint. I
hope you're using the Quartermaster facilities there at the airport.
That will be a big savings during the war

January 28, 1942
Mindanao, Philippine Islands

This is January 28, and we have been having a few days of
much better weather here now. The house I live in is pretty close
to the Agusan River. It is warm, but not as bad for mosquitos as
the other place we were living. We are using the upstairs, which is
drier than the ground floor.

We sent 60 of the penal colony prisoners we have here upriver
today to do some work. They came to me telling me that they
didn't want to go up the river, "Sir." So after one of them had been
told to get back on the boat three times, I had to give him a feel of
my pistol on his jaw. After that, there was no more noise about not
wanting to go. I just slapped him with it. He can make the trip in
good shape. Many times they don't want to do a lot of things.
They're scared of the Japs, and they're scared of the river. We just
have to make them do it. Usually a little stern talk soldier-style will
get the job done.

I have my regiment pretty well set now. There is always so
much work to do, so many things to look after all the time. We
have to make preparations against anything that possibly could
happen. It sure keeps me busy all the time. It looks like now we
will get things pretty well in hand real soon. About the actual
things going on in other parts of the world, I don't know very
much. We have only filtered down news that comes over the radio.
What we hear now seems to indicate that we are doing all right
everywhere.

You all sure would get a kick out of my job, and all that I do
in a day's time. I'm kept busy doing so many different things that I
wonder if I'm looking after my regiment in the best manner.

I have to see that the civilians have some rice to eat. See that
the governor stays on the job. See that the fishermen keep working. See that the evacuees are checked over, watch for deserting
soldiers, keep peace and order within the area. See that the
treasurer gets a boat ride to get some more money for the local
government. See that motor transportation is used as intended.
Check up on the boats coming in and going out. Look after what
we call "local security." Supervise the training of the regiment, plan
all the defenses and see that they are in order. Read and evaluate
all information on the enemy. Check on means of communications
and their secrecy. Keep the Constabulary under control and

observation, as well as labor battalion. These are just some of the things I have looked after today. Tomorrow the problems will be different, but interesting, too. I am really having quite a time. When I get home I'll be able to tell you all the details, and some of the strange things I have learned during my short time over here.

We had another air alarm here today. There were four planes, but they were high and far away. I couldn't tell if they were ours or the enemy. I have seen many enemy planes since I have been on these islands. So far they have not attacked. Their flights are getting farther and farther apart. I expect they will cease pretty soon. I believe now we are really after the little boys from Tokyo.

I sure would give anything for some letters from you all. I'd like to hear how you're getting along. I'll be looking for some mail on the first boat that comes straight across.

I think the hardest part of soldiering over here is that we can't have our mail. The communication is rotten. This is one time the postal system has broken down completely, together with the Quartermaster Corps that lost my wardrobe trunk.

These are my pet peeves. This is all for today. More in a day or so.

February 8, 1942
Roswell, New Mexico
Letter Returned Undeliverable

Dear Daddy,
Mother works at the uso. I bought a war bond at school. Grandaddy has a new suit and girlfriend. It is brown. I wish you would come home and fix my swing.

Love, Betty

February 8, 1942
Mindanao, Philippine Islands

A day or so gets to be Sunday again. Colonel Castlemaine was by last evening and said he thought he could get a letter mailed to the States for me. I'm going to get this letter out today with the chance that you may have it one of these days. In a few days I'll try another radiogram. I'm sure anxious to hear from you. After all it has been a long time. I know you are just as [anxious for this to be over as I am].

My official notification of promotion came through by radio. I don't know as yet from when I rank, but I guess it doesn't matter. Now the situation is that I can also be promoted to temporary rank of full colonel on account of my assignment. I expect to have that one of these days, too. I don't think this has to come from Washington like the other did.

I'll sure be glad when I can get out of these islands. It can't be over too soon to suit me. Next best thing would be to be with American soldiers again. Things are looking better over here, I think. I sure have been busy. I don't think you could believe all I have to do. A blackout won't bother me, because I'm ready for bed at dark. I've forgotten what any kind of nightlife would be like. All of us American officers are the same. We don't have time to do any running around together. We don't receive our pay over here, and if we did, I don't see anything I want to buy.

I've about had to give up my bad habits, too. Like smoking, because we have trouble finding any tobacco we can use. My finicky eating habits, too, are gone. There isn't any choice about food. Some of the things we have over here will sure be out of date when I get home.

The natives are content with three items of rations: rice, sugar, and salt. They will eat two heaping mess-kit pans full at one meal, and more if it's available. I think it is for them like our breakfast foods are for us. We notice that the natives from certain sections of the islands that eat only rice are smaller in size than those who mix a little corn with their foods.

The vegetation everywhere grows rank, and everywhere is nearly like a jungle to begin with. There are always many kinds of spiders, insects walking and flying, and all kinds of blight that seems to be on everything. There's no pest control. I don't know what all they could grow if they had some method of it. But such is life over here.

There is an average of two planes a day over here, but mostly they are so high we can't tell whose they are. Or the clouds keep us from seeing them. But we always hear them. My outfit is not un-familiar with enemy dive bombers and all attack methods used. But they sure are bum shots.

I'm going upriver in a few days to do some reorganizing

and inspection work. I'll be up there a few weeks. The colonel seems to want me to go up there for awhile. I worry about who will do all the things I am doing now here. It will be some kind of vacation for me away from all this. Things got kind of messed up while he was up there last week. So I'll go see what the problem is and get it under control.

I know you all wonder about things. I can only tell you a little. I'll let you know all the details when I can write about them. But we want all our information protected from unauthorized persons. I have quite a collection of unusual letters, messages, and photos. I'll bring them back with me. Some will be kept as a record for future reference since before all of this is over, there will be some officers in quite a jam for doing things that are not according to regulations or customs. Some haven't done the things they should have. But that isn't my worry. It's the Army's worry. I have all I can do to look after my outfit. I'm glad I'm not responsible for supplies, or worse, for the NON-SUPPLIES which we desperately should have, but don't get. When they begin to check up, it will be interesting to see where some of the experts land.

I'm just fine, and doing as well as can be. The filling came out of my front tooth, and [I have lost some weight. We are short of a lot of things we need, but at that we are getting by. There is a lot of griping, but mostly in fun. We are just doing our job until the forces arrive to get us out].

February 14, 1942
Roswell, New Mexico

Letter Returned Undeliverable as "Moved to New Assignment"

Dear Daddy,
I made you a Valentine. It is red. Mean boys chase me home from school. Jeannie has a boyfriend. He doesn't chase her. We ate fried chicken at the Victory Cafe. My doll is pretty. Bounce bit Mr. Lowe, but not hard. Please come home and bring me a present.

Love, Betty

April 5, 1942, Easter Sunday

Mindanao, Philippine Islands

Today is Easter Sunday. I'm over in a part of the country that I like much better than the jungles. It really looks like some parts of the West here. I was a member of the General Court-Martial, (the president, in fact) and we have finished up the trial. I'm still traveling around quite a bit, but over here I get to see a lot of officers I have known quite a while, and we are getting in a little visiting.

Here is a new address:

> Lt. Colonel Arden R. Boellner
> A.P.P. NO. 309 c/o Postmaster
> San Francisco

I'm feeling fine. Just somewhat homesick, otherwise okay.

My love to you all always, Your daddy

April 12, 1942
Cagayan Province, Mindanao, Philippine Islands

My darling Betty, Jeannie, Hazel, and Dad:

This is Sunday, and today has been a day of some activity by the planes, both ours and the Japs. There hasn't been much news the last few days, and we have been as busy as can be from here. From what I hear, I don't think I can send any more radiograms to you all the way I have been doing it before. I'll watch for the first chance though, to get one off to you. I'm doing fine, doing all right. I keep pretty busy all the time. There's never a time when I don't have something to do.

I have seen some action and now we are waiting for the assistance to get us out and finish up this business over here. To us it seems like it has been an awfully long time getting here. But, no doubt, there are a lot of things that have to be considered. I hope that when they do get started, they will be able to do it all up in short order.

I'm getting used to not having news from home. But that's no sign I wouldn't give a lot to have a few letters. When I do hear though, I'll appreciate them even more.

April 14, 1942
Cagayan Province, Mindanao, Philippine Islands

April 14 is starting out a rainy day, which is the first I have known since being here.

Yesterday was another exciting day. We saw a lot of air activity, and to see that we have air support gives us a thrill. Will have to give you all the details later. I have so many things to tell you about. It will take some time to do the whole job. Now we don't want anything to get out that might be of interest to the Japs. We try, and always have a surprise available for them.

I have a new job now, and am no longer in the jungles. I sure do like the change, too, even if it did make some of them mad when I asked to make the change. You find strange folks in the Army, just like everywhere else.

I hope that all of you are fine, and not missing me too much. I'm sure of one thing, and that is that you all have learned to get along without me hanging around all the time. Not that I wouldn't like to be there with you all. As soon as this business is over, I will get back with you again. At least everyone will agree I sure have done some traveling in the last few months. It gets to be some task. .

It's later in the day. It sure has been raining, but it is letting up a little this evening.

Betty, I'm sending this letter to you dear, and you be sure to let your ma and sis read it too. You will have to tell the folks you heard from your Daddy, and that he is feeling fine. I hope you are saving my Christmas present for me, and haven't eaten it all up by now. It's a good thing they don't have candy over here. There is a little ant that can get into anything sweet and always does. Also, it is too warm for chocolate. There are no iceboxes like you all have to keep things in.

You would find most things over here very strange. You would have a time getting used to them. Some places I have been none of the children wear clothes. Some places only a shirt. But it is warm and they don't get cold. But they sure do get dirty.

I haven't seen anything of paper dolls since I saw yours. In fact, youngsters over here don't have toys to play with. They really don't know much about playing. But they sure do know how to carry things. Everyone going anywhere is carrying something, usually on their head. I hope you have been keeping up your practice of carrying the pasteboard box on your head without spilling it off, so you can carry things properly too, if you ever come here.

I've been losing a few clothes here, and am getting pretty low on some things. I was able to pick up a pair of shoes. It isn't anything serious about the clothes, but when I get home I'll have to get that old brown suit I left there out of the closet, for I don't have any civilian clothes. What I had was left in Manila. I don't think I can get those back.

I may have to quit smoking altogether. Cigarettes are sure hard to get, as well as matches. There is nothing whatsoever for sale here. Money is just a nuisance. I spend a little for laundry. I don't believe I spend an average of 50 cents per week over here, including laundry.

April 15, 1942
Cagayan Province, Mindanao, Philippine Islands

Yesterday was a really rainy day. It rained most of the day and the wind blew hard, and blew water right through the walls of these houses, or maybe I should say through the holes in the walls. Everything got wet.

Just as I finished up the first page of this letter the Japs came over with two planes, and gave us another show by dropping four "eggs." From what I saw, where I was a few days ago wouldn't be a very healthy place. I just hope I can stay one jump ahead of them when they do their bombing. It's something to watch, even after all I've seen.

April 17, 1942
Cagayan Province, Mindanao, Philippine Islands

We have had a little more excitement around. Have been very busy, but even at that, it isn't so bad.

While I think of it, like I wrote before, when I start back home I want you to get Santa Fe passes for all of you, round trip tickets, and for me a single pass from wherever I land. If it should be in San Francisco we can meet there, or if better, in Los

Angeles. At this time I don't know if it might not be New York. I
want you to know what I have in mind when the time comes.

I hope I'm still the "Watch Inspector" at the store back there. I
am wondering if our artisans, Clare and Lorenza, aren't in the service by now. Anyway, tell them all hello for me.

Dad - you would really have a time with all the bugs and insects that are here, all eating something, or each other. The people
here don't seem to notice them much, but just let them eat
everything up and see if there is anything left for them.

Around our nipa hut are about ten avocado trees. They remind me of a pear tree, but the foliage is greener. The trees are
heavy and about 20 feet high. There is a banana nut and pistachio,
and many fruits we are not familiar with. I'm going to arrange to
have some seeds and flowers sent back to you. I hope you're not
having to work too hard at the store. I know you know that I want
you to do just what you want.

Betty—you tell Judge McGhee, and Willis, and Doc Fall that
I haven't received the saddle yet. Maybe it is with my wardrobe
trunk. See if they can check up on the shipment from the home
end. Tell Willis he better have his checkbook ready and we'll go to
a men's furnishing store. I still think my wardrobe trunk might
turn up some place in storage. But the things in it are probably
ruined by moisture, or heat or something else (like insects). Maybe
it's in Australia.

We hear Round-the-World broadcasts from San Francisco's
Fairmont Hotel, sent out, I believe, early in the morning, and we
have it here in the evening. That is all the outside news we get.
Sometimes there is so much interference that we don't get that. So
you can see our news sure is limited.

There are no magazines or newspapers published here. All the
issues one can find are 1937–41, so it is good that we don't have to
have these things like we think we do. I have learned that there are
a lot of things I used to think were necessary that I can do without
over here. But I'm still hoping to catch up some of these days.

I'm wondering about things at home. I'll bet everyone who
amounts to anything sure is keeping busy these days to help get
this war out of the way. I'm sure that many I know there are in the
service now. I'm sure anxious to know about all these things as
soon as I can.

I still think it should be part of the duty of some politicians I
know to have to go to the field with the Army, where nice talk

Lieutenant-Colonel Arden R. Boellner

Lieutenant-Colonel Arden R. Boellner of Roswell (above) was last heard from in a letter which he wrote his wife from the Philippines, dated April 29th, when he reported he was fine.

Arden Boellner, now 44 years old, served in the first world war after graduating from N. M. M. I., but the war ended while he was still waiting to be sent abroad. He was honorably discharged as a First Lieutenant and ever since the close of the last war he served as a Reserve Officer, working up to the rank of Major, which he held for seven years prior to the time he was called to active service in the army on July 21, 1941. This time, he was quickly sent abroad, going to the Philippines last October after being stationed a short time at Fort Huachuca, Ariz., and participating in the army maneuvers in Louisiana. His promotion to Lieutenant-Colonel was received last December, about the time the United States entered the war. He served on the Philippines during the entire time the islands were being attacked by the Japs.

Arden Boellner was born in Leon, Kansas, but the family moved to Roswell when he was five years old and he has lived here ever since, taking an active part in community affairs and devoting much time and effort to his duties as a Reserve Officer. Before he was called to active service in the army he was associated with his father, L. B. Boellner, in the operation of the Boellner Jewelry Store.

Lieutenant-Colonel Boellner, known as Arden to his many friends, is one of Roswell's real heroes of this war. He spent nearly a quarter of a century in study and training so as to be of the greatest possible service to his country in just such an emergency as the one for which he was called. Roswell is proud of him and the entire community is joining with his family in the hope of his safe return when victory is won.

Roswell newspaper highlight of a local hero. (Courtesy of *Roswell Daily Record*.)

doesn't help. I sure have learned something of the political setup over here. I believe it is very true that this is even worse here in some places, but this war will cure a big part of it, and I mean they will get the cure for sure.

You probably wonder why I don't give you the news from here in my letters. First, I don't know much about what is going on, except for right around me, and then we have to be careful what we put in letters that might fall into enemy hands.

Bill Rogers is in Cebu. That's the last I heard from him. McClenahan is there with him. I imagine they are okay. We don't have any news from Cebu.

April 17, 1942
Cagayan Province, Mindanao, Philippine Islands

My darlings:

I'll write this last page with a pen so you won't get too tired of the typewriting. I'm going to try to get this letter out today. And try again in another week with another letter. I want to assure you that I am fine, and loving you with all my heart, all the time, and thinking about you a lot.

I'll be very glad when this is over and I can get back. But I also think that we have to get this job done, and done very well before it is time to leave.

I've thought about what I expected to do over here, with reference to what I've actually done, and it doesn't fit together at all. For I have done most of the things I never expected to do when I came over here.

By the way, I think I've lost a little weight, and a filling out of my tooth. That's all the personal things missing.

You all be sweet and love me lots, and keep up the good work.

Betty, you keep on being a good soldier. Best regards to all others. I love you always,

                                        Your Daddy, Arden

Invasion of the Cagayan Sector: May 2–11, 1942

Report of Operations, 93rd Infantry

Near twilight, six Japanese transports and two cruisers were sighted entering Macajalar Bay. All of the regiments were alerted. They stood by until 3:30 A.M. on May 3, 1942.

Orders were received to move a battalion by truck to the Alae position. The battalion was in position by 7:30 A.M. Two hours later Commanding General Sharp ordered riflemen to the vicinity of Km. #19 to protect both flanks of the 2.95 Field Artillery Gun Detachment. One section of .50-caliber machine guns were to be put in defiled position about 400 yards northeast of the demolition of the Sayre Highway. These units remained in position until about 7:30 P.M. During the afternoon the .50-caliber machine guns fired on a group of ten Japanese bicyclists and on an enemy plane overhead.

The remainder of the 93rd Infantry was moved from Libona to the Alae position. During this time, the CPY at Del Monte was moved to Dalirig. The 62nd Infantry was to go into position on the Mangima Canyon. The 93rd was to be a covering force for withdrawal of the 81st Filipino Army, and the 61st Filipino Army. At Casa Manana orders were issued that the demolition work could begin.*

Six available trucks moved supplies to Dalirig. Demolition was then destroying Libona, Santa Fe, Camp 12, Camp 17, Camp 28, and Camp 30. All bridges between Sycip's Ranch and Libona and the bridges across the Agusan River were being blown.

At Alae, between 2:30 A.M. and 6 A.M. chaos and haste resulted in many of the bridges being burned out before all the transportation had

---

*Report of Operations of USAFFE and USFIP in the Philippine Islands, 1941–42, Historical Manuscript File, Headquarters, 93rd Infantry Regiment, John C. Goldtrap, Major 57th Infantry, Commanding.

Top: Del Monte Air Field shortly before Pearl Harbor. These B-17s, B-18s, and one cargo-passenger transport comprised the air strength on Mindanao at that time. (Courtesy of Walt Regehr, Fifth Air Base Group Association.) *Bottom:* Del Monte, prior to first air attack. Note the sandbagged gun emplacements at left. Antiaircraft defense consisted of water and air-cooled .50-caliber machine guns. Some were cannibalized from wrecked B-17s. (Courtesy of Walt Regehr, Fifth Air Base Group Association.)

Top: The road once traveled from Cagayan to Del Monte Airfield, Mindanao, 1942. (Courtesy of Walt Regehr, Fifth Air Base Group Association.) *Bottom:* This is the type of terrain that needed defending, May 1942. This is probably the Agusan River that bordered Del Monte to the north and west. (Courtesy of Walt Regehr, Fifth Air Base Group Association.)

Top: Del Monte Air Base, Mindanao, 1941–42. This B-17 carcass was bullet-ridden by the Japanese. It was moved nearly every night to another part of the field. The Japanese used it for strafing practice. It might be interesting to know how many "kills" were claimed by their pilots. (Courtesy of Walt Regehr, Fifth Air Base Group Association.) *Bottom:* Del Monte Airfield Bivouac Area, 1941–42. (Courtesy of Walt Regehr, Fifth Air Base Association.)

been moved safely to the rear. The last units of the 61st Filipino Army passed the Alae junction at 5 A.M. The second battalion of the 93rd Infantry withdrew from the Alae position to Puntian by way of the CPY road to Sankanan.

At 6 A.M. on May 4, the 93rd Infantry, Colonel William F. Dalton commanding, withdrew its third and first battalions along essentially the same route, following the Sayre Highway to Diklom Ranch, to CPR road, Sankanan, to Puntian, a southern loop on the highway. All units carried out what demolitions they could, including the Del Monte dugout, and the CPR dugout, which contained maps showing troop dispositions, and documents marked "Secret," and "Confidential." There was no sign of the enemy at this time.

The march to Puntian of about 30 kilometers was difficult, as most equipment had to be carried by hand. The withdrawal order had come too soon for the men to be fed breakfast. The barrio Puntian was outposted. The troops rested and bivouacked until the last elements arrived about 11 A.M. on May 5.

At Mangima Canyon the 1st Battalion occupied the right subsector, the 2nd Battalion the left. The 3rd Battalion was held in reserve at Puntian. The right boundary was the junction of the Mangima Canyon and the Anibong River. The 61st was on our right. The left boundary was Licoan. The defensive frontage of the 93rd Infantry Regiment was 11.75 miles.

At 9 A.M. Company L and one section of heavy machine guns was sent to Sankanan to get rice and sugar from the bodega.

The enemy was quiet on May 5, 6, and 7. Supply was a problem in our sector. The men were tired and anxious. But morale was high. We waited.

At 5:45 A.M. on May 8, the outpost at Sankanan was fired on by eight machine guns from the West Bank of the Sankanan Canyon. Ten trucks of the enemy were sighted unloading on the Sankanan-Tankulan Road. They opened fire with eight machine guns and four mortars. Their fire was high and ineffective.

Captain Burlando with one platoon was sent to personally give withdrawal orders to two platoons of Company I. He could not locate the other platoons which were hiding in *cogan* grass. One of our machine guns was hit by enemy mortar. Our second gun was captured. The wounded gunner of our captured machine gun killed one Japanese officer and two soldiers with his bolo knife and escaped.

A section of mortars was sent forward to support Company I and Company L, which were being attacked by five companies of the enemy. With our mortars in position, the enemy took cover. His forward advance and flanking movement was halted.

Reinforcements were ordered up to support our troops. A skirmish line was formed. A counterattack forced the enemy to withdraw to the north. The machine gun of the 1st Battalion opened fire on the enemy at a range of 1,000 yards, inflicting heavy casualties. The enemy withdrew about one kilometer to the northwest with his right flank resting on the Mangima Canyon. Companies I, L, and C, with one platoon of machine guns and one mortar supporting, occupied this position. Our morale was exceedingly high at this time.

By noon on May 8, it was evident that any enemy attack would be in the vicinity of the 61st Filipino Army and the 93rd Infantry. The 1st Battalion was ordered to move into the right half of the right subsector. The 2nd Battalion was moved from Kocoan to Old Ocasion, four kilometers south of Puntian. By 1 P.M. there was a lull in the fighting. Only sporadic shots were being fired.

All battalions immediately sent out reconnaissance patrols, with the 1st Battalion going into the bottom of Mangima Canyon to prevent enemy infiltration.

At 3:30 P.M. truck loads of the enemy were sighted on a road leading east from Sankanan. This road had been blocked by the destruction of four of our own trucks. Two enemy trucks were stopped about 1,200 yards from the L Company position. These were fired upon by our machine guns. Our mortar opened up on the six remaining trucks, crippling the last truck. The other seven trucks quickly withdrew to the north. The enemy was observed loading dead soldiers into their trucks.

Thirty minutes later the enemy launched a weak attack against the position of the 1st Battalion, which was repulsed with rifle and machine gun fire. Thinking that we occupied a position east of the Anibong River, the enemy laid down a mortar barrage to the rear of the 1st Battalion position. A Lieutenant Williams had been sent towards Mangoa to reconnoiter an assembly area for a battalion, and was apparently trapped with the mortar barrage. His body was found the next day.

There was no further enemy activity on May 8. During the evening orders were received that our right boundary would be extended to the Dalirig Hill Mass. This meant moving one battalion to occupy the left half of the sector of the 61st Filipino Army. The 1st and 2nd Battalions were already in position, the 3rd Battalion, which was withdrawing to the Mangima Canyon arrived in Puntian at 1:30 A.M.

on May 9. This unit had been in action for two days and was exhausted. They were fed, and extra ammunition was issued. At 3 A.M. they moved out to occupy their new position in the vicinity of Nangca. No reconnaissance had been possible during the hours of darkness. In spite of the difficulties, the 3rd Battalion had occupied the position by 6 A.M.

A few minutes later the enemy launched an attack against the 1st Battalion in an attempt to cross the Mangima Canyon at the Nangca Trail. The attack was repulsed by rifle and machine gun fire. At 7 A.M. about 300 of the enemy were massed on the west side of the Mangima Canyon opposite the left of the 3rd Battalion. We expected an attack but it never materialized. Instead, the enemy sent out snipers to infiltrate our lines.

The 1st Battalion was harassed by snipers from 8 A.M. until 3 P.M. By changing his original defensive line from a north-south direction at the junction of the Mangima Canyon and Anibong River, so that his lines faced west, north and east, and by sending out small aggressive patrols, Captain Finigan was able to silence a total of nine snipers.

On May 9 at about noon, reserve snipers were in the rear of the 3rd Battalion. Captain Burlando sent out patrols and was successful in silencing the snipers, which had, we believed, infiltrated through a gap between the 61st Filipino Army and the 93rd Infantry. We did not have sufficient troops to have this gap occupied. Most other enemy activity ceased, except for the periodic disturbance by snipers, who were taken care of in a few minutes after an initial shot.

We received orders to withdraw about 5:30 P.M. to Sumilao. There we were to organize a defensive position on the Kulaman River. The message also stated that the 93rd Infantry might be put on its own. By now we all could see the handwriting on the wall.

Orders were issued to withdraw the regiments and to occupy the Kulaman River position. The regiment was to withdraw in the following order: 2nd Battalion, Headquarters Battalion, 1st Battalion, and the 3rd Battalion. At about 6 o'clock in the evening, the enemy laid down a rolling mortar and light artillery barrage on the right sector of the 1st Battalion, which lasted about an hour and a half.

The officers and the enlisted men of the 1st Battalion conducted themselves admirably. They remained in their foxholes, and one machine gun went into a slight defiladed position, silencing one enemy mortar. Three men were wounded and one machine gun was damaged.

The *surrender ceremony*, May 11, 1942. Troops gathered at Malaybalay. Photo presumably recovered from Japanese officer when hostilities ended. (Courtesy of Walt Regehr, Fifth Air Base Group Association.)

The 2nd Battalion passed through Puntian en route to Sumilao about 7 P.M. It was followed immediately by the Headquarters Battalion. The 1st Battalion passed Puntian at 10:30 P.M. The 3rd Battalion arrived in Puntian at 1 A.M. When we arrived in Sumilao at 3:00 A.M. on May 10, we were informed of the proposed surrender. We ordered all battalions into Sumilao to bivouac. The last element arrived in Sumilao at 6:00 P.M.

The troops were fed, the regiment was formed. All arms and ammunition were turned in per orders. There were approximately 1,500 members of the 93rd Infantry present in this formation.

At 5:00 P.M. on May 10, 1942, as per our orders, we accompanied Colonel Dalton to contact the Commander of the Japanese Forces, at which time the American forces were surrendered

At 11:00 A.M. on May 11 the 93rd Infantry moved out for Malaybalay They marched 57 kilometers in 28 hours, entering that

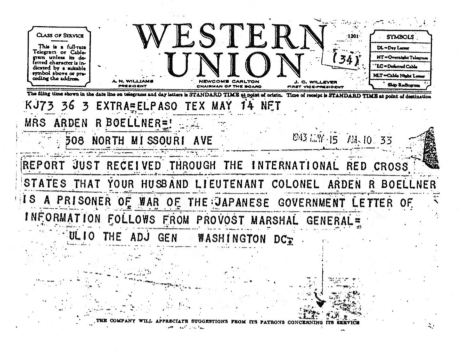

CLASS OF SERVICE

This is a full-rate Telegram or Cablegram unless its deferred character is indicated by a suitable symbol above or preceding the address.

WESTERN UNION

A. N. WILLIAMS
PRESIDENT

NEWCOMB CARLTON
CHAIRMAN OF THE BOARD

J. C. WILLEVER
FIRST VICE-PRESIDENT

SYMBOLS

DL = Day Letter
NT = Overnight Telegram
LC = Deferred Cable
NLT = Cable Night Letter
Ship Radiogram

The filing time shown in the date line on telegrams and day letters is STANDARD TIME at point of origin. Time of receipt is STANDARD TIME at point of destination

KJ73 36 3 EXTRA=ELPASO TEX MAY 14 NFT

MRS ARDEN R BOELLNER=!

508 NORTH MISSOURI AVE   1943 MAY 15 AM 10 33

REPORT JUST RECEIVED THROUGH THE INTERNATIONAL RED CROSS
STATES THAT YOUR HUSBAND LIEUTENANT COLONEL ARDEN R BOELLNER
IS A PRISONER OF WAR OF THE JAPANESE GOVERNMENT LETTER OF
INFORMATION FOLLOWS FROM PROVOST MARSHAL GENERAL=
ULIO THE ADJ GEN   WASHINGTON DC=

THE COMPANY WILL APPRECIATE SUGGESTIONS FROM ITS PATRONS CONCERNING ITS SERVICE

Telegram notification of POW status from War Department, May 1943.

camp as a unit. The 93rd Infantry carried out every mission that was assigned. I have nothing but admiration for my troops.*

*Report of Operations of USAFFE and USFIP in the Philippine Islands, 1941–42, Historical Manuscript File, Headquarters, 93rd Infantry Regiment, John C. Goldtrap, Major 57th Infantry, Commanding.

Aftermath of Surrender:
May 1942–June 1944

The small military outpost of Camp Casisang in the foothills of the Malaybalay Mountains, a few miles north of the barrio of the same name, was the collecting point for the units on Mindanao. The units accounted for about 1,100 men and officers of the surrendered American Army, the 93rd Infantry Regiment soldiers among them. Arden Boellner, Colonel William F. Dalton, and Colonel Wade Killen were assigned to share a nipa hut.

As the men settled in at Camp Casisang, following the Official Surrender Formation, they tried to sort out all the confusion and shock of the last few weeks. What had really happened to bring it about? Few knew about General Wainwright's message to General Sharp on May 6, relinquishing Wainwright's command of the Visayan-Mindanao to Sharp. But most had heard General Wainwright's Manila broadcast on May 7, ordering all the troops in the Philippine archipelago to lay down their arms and obey the surrender order. One officer claimed to have been present in General Sharp's headquarters when he radioed MacArthur in Melbourne for clarification of Wainwright's order. MacArthur had fired back that they were "to separate the forces into small elements and initiate guerilla operations,"* adding that General Sharp had been given full authority to make field decisions. Some of the men grumbled, they knew for certain that the "Japs had been holding a gun at Wainwright's head when he made the broadcast from Manila." But the decision had been an order. Some of the men were bewildered, others openly angry.

Rumors spread in camp that a prisoner exchange was being arranged. That was what they wanted to hear: Uncle Sam hadn't abandoned them. It would be different here, it wouldn't be like it was at

*Louis Morton, U.S. Army in World War II: The Fall of the Philippines (Washington, D.C.: Center of Military History), p. 575.

65

American prisoners of war at forced labor, Malaybalay, Mindanao, summer 1942. (Courtesy of Walt Regehr, Fifth Air Base Group Association.)

Wake Island. Meanwhile, they could make the best of it. There was food to eat from their own Army stockpiles. They had been allowed to keep most of their personal gear. One or two of the men had radios. The Fifth Air Base Group, numbering about 1,000 men, was nick-named the "Footlocker Fifth" by fellow prisoners who admired the grand style of their fully equipped footlockers. This group had been sent to Mindanao to build and maintain satellite airfields farther to the south, as well as the strategic Del Monte Airfield. Some of these men had arrived on Mindanao just in time to surrender.

The Japanese, awaiting orders from Tokyo, appeared accommo-dating, curious. The camp commander ordered work details for maintenance and vegetable farming. The officers complied and pro-vided enlisted men for the chores.

A choral group, the "Mindanao Melodeers" gathered in the eve-nings to rehearse, much to the amusement of the Japanese. The men swapped stories, griped, predicted their chances of getting back to the States. The new enemy was boredom. They waited, trying to com-prehend the rules of a new war, the war fought behind barbed wire.

Orders from Tokyo arrived at Camp Casisang in late summer.

Colonel Dalton, Colonel Killen, and Lt. Colonel Boellner lived in this nipa shack, Camp Casisang, Malaybalay, Mindanao, August 1942. (Smuggled photo, courtesy of Colonel William F. Dalton, 93rd Infantry Regiment.)

The officers with rank of colonel and above were to be transferred north for shipment to Japan. With the news a cloud of despair settled over the camp. Those designated for transport began to pack up. They said goodbye to fellow officers, they shook hands with each of the men they had commanded.

Colonel William F. Dalton said goodbye to Arden Boellner, his executive officer. Boellner gave his commander his business card from civilian life, from Boellner's Jewelry Store, with the address of his hometown in New Mexico. On the back of the card Arden wrote his wife's name, Hazel. They promised each other that whichever one of them returned home first would contact the other's family. Colonel Dalton also carefully concealed two matchbook-size snapshots taken with Boellner's camera of Boellner, Colonel Wade Killen, and himself, which he hoped to smuggle from the camp.*

American POWs lined the sides of the dirt road to watch their officers being loaded into trucks. It was September 6, 1942. They stood

*From letter from Colonel William F. Dalton, 1946.

Colonel Dalton and Arden Boellner, at Camp Casisang, the latter part of August 1942. Foothills of the Malaybalay Mountains in the distance. (Courtesy of Colonel William F. Dalton.)

at attention as the trucks rolled out, carrying the officers they had served. Silent, each man struggling with his own thoughts, they watched the trucks disappear. It was a terrible day.

In October 1942, Camp Casisang was ordered closed. The remaining POWs were taken by truck to Cagayan. They passed the abandoned Del Monte Airfield overgrown with weeds and grass. They saw the bombed-out shell of the Philippine Packing Company, a large

Top: A photo of the Del Monte Philippine Packing Corporation cannery on the beach at Bugo. This cannery had been shelled by a Japanese submarine. (Courtesy of Walt Regehr, Fifth Air Base Group Association.) *Bottom:* Abandoned bivouac area, Del Monte Airfield, 1942. Note the rugged mountains in the background. (Courtesy of Walt Regehr, Fifth Air Base Group Association.)

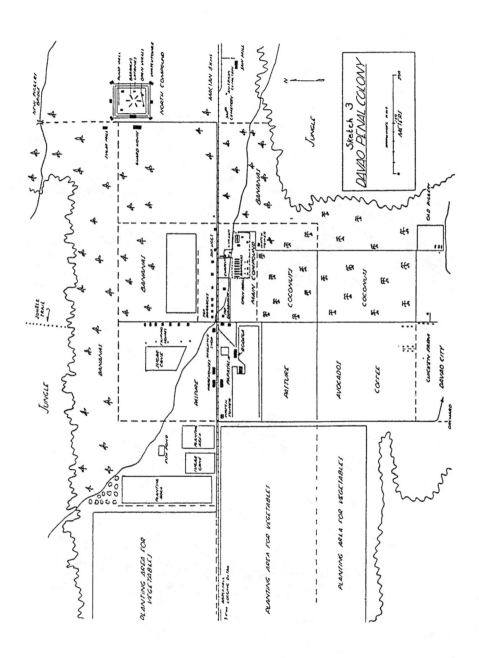

Sketch 3
DAVAO PENAL COLONY

APPROXIMATE SCALE
METERS

warehouse where many American civilians had been employed before the war. At the Cagayan docks there was a long, thirsty wait, the first of many to come. Finally, they were herded aboard an old freighter with rusted, painted-over lettering. Some of the POWs speculated that the ship had been British. The Japanese had built shelves on the deck for cargo. The POWs were ordered below.

The course was east through Surigao Straits to Davao Bay, through the narrow passage between Samal Island to Mindanao. The men had canteens full of water and their own food, from hoarded supplies. The hatches were left open, and though heavily guarded, the men had access to the deck for use of the latrine, made only of box boards set on planks beyond the rail of the ship. Four days after leaving Cagayan, the old freighter anchored at a lumber dock, called Lasang Dock.

Another roll call was taken, and still eating from their own rations, the men were marched the 15 miles to Davao Penal Colony, a rugged march even for fit men, exhausting for the POWs already showing early ravages of malnutrition and tropical diseases. Hot, thirsty, weary, they walked into the compound after nightfall.

The Japanese had removed most of the long-term convicts occupying the farm prison. Only about 150 remained to make room for the arriving POWs. Eight barracks in the shape of long barns, grim, sagging buildings with wood floors and badly in need of paint, sat on a three-mile compound surrounded by jungle. The grounds were filled by coconut and banana groves, sugar cane fields, pastures for carabao, a piggery, a fish pond, and a fresh-water well. A small narrow gauge railroad bisected the camp. The POWs looked around them with some assurance that there was going to be food to eat.

The American prisoners from the islands of Cebu were arriving too. Many of them had been friends in the States. Many of them had made the voyage to the Philippines together. They had plenty of stories to tell each other.

One Japanese guard, Mr. Nisamura, who always carried a riding crop, made himself immediately known to the prisoners who tagged him "Simon Legree." In the weeks to come many of the men would feel that riding crop across their backs and faces. Another well-remembered guard hummed unlikely melodies such as "The Merry Widow Waltz," "Red Wing," "Yankee Doodle Dandy," and "Onward Christian

Opposite: **Sketch of Davao Penal Colony. (Courtesy of John McGee, reprinted from** *Rice and Salt,* **San Antonio, Naylor Company, 1962.)**

Top: Approach to Davao Penal Colony, Mindanao. A good view of the parade ground with barracks and mango trees in the background. (Photograph by Lt. Glenn L. Nordin. Courtesy of Carl Nordin, Fifth Air Base Group Association.) *Bottom:* A building outside the compound of Davao Penal Colony used by Japanese guards. (Photograph by Lt. Glenn L. Nordin. Courtesy of Carl Nordin, Fifth Air Base Group Association.)

Top: Non-comm barracks at Davao Penal Colony. Protestant church services were sometimes held under these trees. (Photograph by Lt. Glenn L. Nordin. Courtesy of Carl Nordin, Fifth Air Base Group Association.) *Bottom:* Area in back of latrines at Davao Penal Colony. "The asterisk marks the spot where a POW was shot through the stomach by a Japanese tower guard. Several of us were on a Sunday stroll when the POW reached down by the fence to pick an edible weed. He got within the meter limit." (Photograph by Lt. Glenn L. Nordin. Courtesy of Carl Nordin, Fifth Air Base Group Association.)

Top: Area in back of the barracks at Davao Penal Colony. This is the area where some POWs had small vegetable gardens. (Photograph by Lt. Glenn L. Nordin. Courtesy of Carl Nordin, Fifth Air Base Group Association.) *Bottom:* Close up view of fence and barracks at Davao Penal Colony, Mindanao. (Photograph by Lt. Glenn L. Nordin. Courtesy of Carl Nordin, Fifth Air Base Group Association.)

Top: Front door, fence, and barracks at Davao Penal Colony, Mindanao Military Prison Camp 2. (Photograph by Lt. Glenn L. Nordin. Courtesy of Carl Nordin, Fifth Air Base Group Association.) *Bottom:* Barracks for American POWs at Davao Penal Colony, Mindanao. (Photograph by Lt. Glenn L. Nordin. Courtesy of Carl Nordin, Fifth Air Base Group Association.)

Top: Kitchen area at Davao Penal Colony, fence made of runway matting. (Photograph by Lt. Glenn L. Nordin. Courtesy of Carl Nordin, Fifth Air Base Group Association.) *Bottom:* Hospital area of Davao for American POWs, Mindanao. (Photograph by Lt. Glenn L. Nordin. Courtesy of Carl Nordin, Fifth Air Base Group Association.)

Soldiers." He carried a bamboo switch, which he was quite adept at using. Still another guard liked a joke or two. One day at the piggery, when a new litter of pigs were snorting about, he prodded one of the Americans with his bayonet, saying, "You the Papa — you the Papa."*

In early November 1942, the first work detail of about 1,000 men arrived at Davao Penal Colony from Camp 3 at Cabanatuan, about 60 miles north of Manila, aboard the *Erie Maru*. It was the first real look at the "Battling Bastards of Bataan," and the "Heroes of Corregidor" that the Americans in the southern islands had had.

The eighth of each month was Imperial Rescript Day, complete with parade and drill and the reading of the Emperor's Document, held high less it be desecrated. The Japanese Major Maeda, commander of the camp, after issuing his formal recitation of camp rules to the ranks of American POWs, looked with disgust at his newly arrived labor force. The men from Cabanatuan were hardly more than walking skeletons.

The men were filthy, most had lice, they were starved and ragged. The Cabanatuan POWs seemed dazed. They had come from the horror of Camp O'Donnell and Cabanatuan to this paradise. The adjustment took time. The Malaybalay prisoners, and those of the southern islands, after the initial shock of seeing their fellow prisoners in such condition, pitched in to share their provisions. The following night after supper, the "Mindanao Melodeers," the choral group formed at Malaybalay, gathered in front of the barracks where the Cabanatuan men were, their ranks facing Major Pritchard. They began to sing, "Honey," "If I Had My Way," "Old Man Noah," and the "Ranger's Song." That night they were singing straight from the heart.

The arrivals from Cabanatuan — some broken physically, some spiritually, most scrawny, ragged, diseased — listened with tears streaming down their haggard faces. Here was something to live for again.†

With the camp at capacity, the POWs settled into a routine day. Most of the officers occupied Barracks 1 and Barracks 2. Boellner was assigned to Barracks 1. He took a bottom bunk, made with sliding doors and screened on all sides. It reminded him a little of a rabbit hutch. The barracks were comparatively uncrowded. Doctors and corpsmen occupied the hospital barracks. Two other barracks were reserved for the sick.

*Alan McCracken, Very Soon Now, Joe (New York: Hobson Book Press, 1947).
† The comments of Kenneth Day, Fifth Air Base Group, from Donald Knox, Death March (New York: Harcourt Brace Jovanovich, 1981).

Compass case belonging to Wayne Lewis's brother, engraved by Arden Boellner at Davao Penal Colony, 1943.

Between Barracks 4 and 5, along the path to the latrines, Boellner set up a small store in an old shed. Here, he repaired timepieces, did engraving for the prisoners, put items for trade or sale on the shelves, mended eyeglasses, even tried his hand at shoe repair. The store became a popular place. Wayne Lewis, one of the 31st Infantry arrivals from Luzon, asked Boellner to engrave a compass case belonging to his brother who had died at Camp O'Donnell. Another fellow prisoner asked him to engrave the lid of his mess kit. He traded some tobacco for the work. Some men came by just to talk, others to trade, some to just look around. It was what Boellner had done best in civilian life—run a store.

Barracks leaders were chosen by ability, not rank. Volunteers for work details fulfilled schedules demanded by the Japanese. One of the most "popular" jobs was rice planting. About 1,000 men rode the small gauge railway five miles out of the camp to "play in the Mactan mud." The work was tedious, filthy, and exhausting, but it was a ride away from the camp. There were always volunteers for "Mactan detail." During the times given for rest, many of the prisoners picked small red peppers for flavoring their tasteless rice. Some caught microscopic fish using bent pins in nearby pools. For some of the men the jungle with its colorful birds, monkeys, and foliage held an odd fascination. There was little to be seen beyond it.

The POWs were given a questionnaire, the only one presented at Davao Penal Colony. On it was the single question: "What did you think of the attack on Pearl Harbor?" The response was one of amusement, but the Japanese were quite serious about it being properly filled out by each man. The questionnaires were collected and graded. The men receiving the highest grades were given an extra ration of rice. No one could ever figure out what criteria had determined the highest scores.*

As the weeks rolled on toward the holidays, the POWs looked forward to a rumored shipment of Red Cross packages to be delivered in time for Christmas. Business was brisk in Boellner's store in anticipation of badly needed items. Each day they watched the road for trucks bringing the packages. Christmas Day arrived. The packages did not.

On Christmas Eve, Major Maeda donned full uniform, a change from the usual underclothing the POWs were accustomed to seeing him in. He gave one package of Japanese cigarettes to each prisoner. There was even a Christmas show, a variety of acts performed by both Japanese and Americans. Filipino women danced an island dance. Candy was given out. The "Mindanao Melodeers" closed the show with a traditional singing of "Silent Night." Christmas Day also brought larger servings of camp food. With thoughts of home, of loved ones, memories of better Christmases foremost in their thoughts, the American POWs at Davao Penal Colony ended their first Christmas, and entered a new year as captives.

The wait was worth it when, in late January, the Red Cross packages arrived. Each POW received two 11-pound packages. The Japanese immediately reduced the camp rations to offset the surplus. A week later, as a bonus, each man was allowed to send a 50-word postcard home. The cards could not be dated, nor could anything be said as to camp location or conditions. Cards were printed with multiple choice replies regarding the prisoner's health, injuries, medical treatment. Three blank lines were left at the bottom of the card for messages. Those who had no family to write to addressed cards to

Interview with Russell Hutchison, 1990.

IMPERIAL JAPANESE ARMY

1. I am interned at Phil Mil Prison Camp No. 2.

2. My health is — excellent; good; fair; poor.

3. I am — injured; sick in hospital; under treatment; not under treatment...

4. I am — improving; not improving; better; well.

5. Please see that all is kept intact.Enjoy best possible.
dont worry.Anxious get home. no word in a year.
                                                    is taken care of.

6. (Re: Family) Sunday Easter.Love all so much.Pray you
all well,strong.Wish were with you.This third card.

7. Please give my best regards to all you always. Am proud.

IMPERIAL JAPANESE ARMY

1. I am interned at Philippine Military Prison Camp No. 2

2. My health is — excellent; good; fair; poor.

3. I am — injured; sick in hospital; under treatment; not under treatment.

4. I am — improving; not improving; better; well.

5. Please see that Hazel Jean Betty are always OK; take care of
                                              Anxious to get
yourself & each other; care for my interests. back home
                                              is taken care of.

6. (Re: Family) Love and thinking you always. This is 5th card
                only way of word to you. No word from you as yet

7. Please give my best regards to store gang and all; hope everything OK

Red Cross POW cards. The fifth card, received September 16, 1943, suggested, "Read II Corinthians: 1st Chapter, Verse 2–14." Verse 8 was most common on POW cards. "For we would not brethren, have you ignorant of our trouble which has come to us in Asia, that we were pressed out of measure, above strength, insomuch that we despaired even of life." The sixth Red Cross card received was sent from Cabanatuan, July 10, 1944 and was received at home on February 27, 1945, Arden Boellner's birthday.

IMPERIAL JAPANESE ARMY

1. I am interned at Philippine Military Prison Camp # 2.

2. My health is — excellent; good; fair; poor.

3. I am — injured; sick in hospital; under treatment; not under treatment.

4. I am — improving; not improving; better; well.

5. Please see that all keep fine. Received undated wire glad all fine doing watch work here keeping busy. Taken care of.

6. (Re: Family) this 6th card only way to get you word. anxious to get home appreciate you all more daily

7. Please give my best regards to all my love always thinking of you

IMPERIAL JAPANESE ARMY

1. I am interned at—Philippine Military Prison Camp No. 2

2. My health is—excellent; good; fair; poor.

3. Message (50 words limit)

This seventh card - only communication allowed. Hope you get them. Pray you are all well. _____ _____ _____ _____
will _____ _____ _____ to get everything new as now am completely out. Think about each of you constantly. All my love to each of you always. _____

Signature

movie stars — Betty Grable, Lana Turner, Dorothy Lamour — or to their congress representatives. Many tried to be creative beyond the rules.

"I feel as well as Albert did when he came to stay," one prisoner wrote. (Albert had been the man's stray dog, who was skin and bones when found.) When questioned about the statement by Japanese

IMPERIAL JAPANESE ARMY

1. I am interned at Phil Mil Prison Camp No. 2

2. My health is — excellent; good; fair; poor.

3. I am—uninjured; sick in hospital; under treatment; not under treatment.

4. I am — improving; not improving; better; well.

5. Please see that insurance business farm hard going-Howden died Dec. Need most things keep all intact. is taken care of.

6. (Re: Family); Look after each other, No word in year wish be home Read 11 Carinthians 1; 2-14 Keep faith hope love you all.

7. Please give my best regards to Hazel, Jeannie, Betty Dad gang all

IMPERIAL JAPANESE ARMY

1. I am interned at—Philippine Military Prison Camp No. 1

2. My health is—excellent; good; fair; poor.

3. Message (50 words limit)

No word as yet. Keep up your spirits as I am doing. Take good care of yourself and all the folks. It has been a long ordeal which I hope will soon end so can be back there. My love to each of you always. This tenth card. Happy birthday Betty.

July 10, 1944   Signature

censors at the camp, the POW told them that Albert was an elderly relative who had come to stay with them. (They couldn't fill him up.) The censors approved the card message.

The soldier's message proved not too far from the truth when the Red Cross packages were empty. The rule of reduced rations prevailed above protests to the Japanese by camp leaders. Food was being grown

IMPERIAL JAPANESE ARMY

1. I am interned at ___Philippine Military Camp No 2___

2. My health is — excellent; good; fair; poor. _So so for now_

3. I am — injured; sick in hospital; under treatment; not under treatment.

4. I am — improving; not improving; better; _well._

5. Please see that ___The daughters to be informed that___
   ___daddy will be home soon . Take care of___ is taken care of.

6. (Re: Family): ___Hope family is in good health & good con___

7. Please give my best regards to ___Happy Birthday to Hazel___

in abundance. But it was being carted from the camp or left to rot. This was the first of many indications of harder days to come.

The escape of ten POWs in April brought a wave of repercussions to the camp. POWs occupying the same barracks with the escapees were moved into isolation in the north compound for 90 days, for "meditation." The entire camp was put on a ration of rice and salt for one week. Filipino employees were dismissed. Japanese guards tightened security. Beatings increased. Any attempt by workers to smuggle even the smallest amount of food into the camp had almost ceased. The risk was too great. The "Mindanao Melodeers," too weak and exhausted to practice, disbanded.

Boellner kept his store intact, though the shelves were mostly empty. He gave instructions in watch repair to those with the energy to listen.* Japanese now brought their watches, eyeglasses, cameras, and shoes to him for repair. Occasionally he was able to trade the work for a little extra rice. The rice was saved in an old Klim can from one of his Red Cross packages, to be divided with his barracks mates.†

In the evenings Boellner sat with Charles Brown on the steps of Barracks 2, playing his part in guarding one of the best-kept secrets at the camp. Inside the deserted Barracks 2 sat Russell Hutchison, who

---

*From a letter from Morris Shoss, 1944.
†From comments of Colonel Cain, 1944.

had ingeniously built a tiny radio from parts salvaged from Japanese radios he had repaired, using the hour hands from an old clock in Arden's shop for the tuner. From Barracks 4 Clyde Ely watched Charles Brown. When Charlie crossed his legs, it was a signal that the guard was coming into the gate. It took 55 seconds for the guard to unlock two gates and walk down the row of barracks. Ely would move out through a side door, lift up the window to Barracks 2 where Russell was operating the radio, and knock. Day, who sat with Russell, would take out the extension cord and unplug the radio. Clyde Ely stayed by the door, took the tube and coil off the radio and put it in his sewing kit. Then he walked off toward the latrine. The closest call came one night when one of the two guard gates was already unlocked. That night the guard made his pass along the barracks in 40 seconds.

During the day only one man, Clyde Ely, knew where the radio was hidden. Some might have guessed, but only Ely knew for sure. Once the hiding place was nearly discovered when a dog, drawn to the scent of corned beef, dug beneath the barracks and exposed the can. It was found in time.

The miraculous little radio picked up broadcasts originating from KTEI in San Francisco, short wave from Australia. The London broadcasts were frustrating—about budgets, The House of Commons, The House of Lords. The best station was Chungking, China, the Armed Forces Radio. Every scrap of news was reported to Colonel Olson. What the senior staff officers felt was "safe news" was filtered among the ranks. When Russell Hutchison had put the finishing touches on his creation, tried the radio for the very first time, and it worked, loud and clear, he turned to look at Colonel Olson.

"Thank God," the Colonel said. And everyone agreed.*

The summer of 1943 dragged by. Men confined to the north compound spent their days in isolation from the rest of the camp, playing chess or bridge "from dark to dark."† The rice detail to Mactan still went out, but the men worked more slowly. They were hungry. The reduced rations were sapping strength from all. More of the men were sick, there was less and less medicine with which to treat the complicated tropical diseases. Guards were in an ugly mood. The smallest infraction of some rule, such as an improper bow to a passing guard, brought a severe beating. Broadcasts on the secret radio told of

*Interview with Russell Hutchison, 1990.
†Ibid.

MacArthur's progress in the Pacific. To the POWs waiting, the progress seemed very slow. Still, the rumors flowed. "Thanksgiving turkey in Albuquerque," became a favorite saying with the POWs from New Mexico.* The theme spread through the camp. One POW tried to compose a song using the theme. The men tried to conquer the hunger pangs that assailed them. They thought always, and first, of food. One incident in the Mactan rice fields proved the point.

The mud was particularly deep and slimy that day following a rain. One of the men, a big strapping man, who by now like the others was mostly bone and sinew, spotted a snake. He grabbed for it. It slithered off. He grabbed again, fell to his stomach and caught it. He drew it to length and snapped off its head. With the body of the snake still wriggling, he took off his hat, curled the snake inside of it, and put his hat back on.

"We'll eat tonight, boys," he grinned. When one of the guards approached to reprimand him, yelling at him in a high shrill voice, the man pointed to the head of the snake lying in the mud.

"You can't insult me — I'm too ignorant," the man told the guard quite solemnly.†

The guard fled. The Japanese were deathly afraid of snakes.

With the approach of Christmas, the Japanese announced that the long-awaited Red Cross shipment would not arrive on schedule. That news, along with another incident, weighed heavily upon the minds of the POWs. An American major who worked in the carpenter shop went berserk and killed a Japanese guard with a hammer. He was taken to be tortured, his screams heard by all for hours from a stockade a good distance away. This news, that a man they felt as sane as most was now dead, brought increasing gloom. To offset the mood, the POWs organized a musical group. They asked the Japanese for music sheets. Shunusuke Wada, the hunchbacked Japanese interpreter was pleased with the idea, and provided the request. Practices began. The orchestra played for the Christmas Eve variety show. The acts lacked the spirit of the previous Christmas, but nonetheless, the POWs enjoyed being entertained, though few could follow the peculiar Japanese melodies. On Christmas Day the *lugao* was a little thicker. The Japanese dispensed some of their Oriental cigarettes. These were smoked with relish, even by true smokers who once despised the taste. The tobacco helped the hunger pangs.*

*Interview with Wayne Lewis, 1989.
†Interview with Russell Hutchison, 1990.

Boellner's name somehow found its way to the December 23, 1943, Tokyo Radio Broadcast, "Humanity Calls," a propaganda broadcast intended to soothe over the atrocity issue reported by Davao escapee Ed Dyess upon his return to freedom. The program offered a little music, then messages from POWs. Official Red Cross messages differed from those picked up and monitored by amateur shortwave radio operators. No official record was kept of amateur messages, but many of the messages were heard by more than one amateur operator. The families mentioned on the broadcasts were located, called, and the message was read to them.

> This is Uzelle D. Walker, U.S. Marines, formerly of Corregidor, Philippine Islands, speaking to Mrs. Clara Walker, El Paso, Texas. "Dear Mother and all, My future . . . getting along. I pray . . . please do not worry yourself as all things must come to an end sometime, and when that time comes . . . Until my return . . . Murray Brown, Tacoma is here. Nothing can be done for my leg until I return. Merrit Christle, Marines is with me, Benjamin Dawe and Ernest Trent are in Nippon. Colonel Boellner in same camp and well. They are not in bad health. Each night I hold you in mind and have made plans. I long dearly to see Mother, Father, Babe, Buster, Pauline. Tell Gerry Anne . . . I wish my friends Merry Christmas. Sincerely, your loving son, . . . Uzelle.*

The secret camp radio reported that MacArthur and Admiral Nimitz were on the move in the Pacific. By February 29 Kwajalien and Eniwetok were secured. Early in March the United States Marines landed at Talasea, New Britain. The battle for Bougainville was still on. Such news helped to overcome the agonizing wait for promised Red Cross packages. This time the men were shorted a package, and some packages were damaged, leaving ruined contents. The Japanese had opened most of them and removed appealing contents. Packages of cigarettes had been opened, and the packaging removed when the Lucky Strike cigarettes changed from their familiar green-and-gold package to the red, white, and blue. Some had patriotic emblems, "Buy War Bonds." The Japanese collected the hundreds of opened cigarettes, dumped them, broken in two, into a box. They gave the box to the senior staff officers to distribute. The camp rice ration that had been reduced the previous January, was again reduced. Food was

Author's collection, 1944–45.

growing short in the Philippines. What had been a short ration for the POWS was fast becoming a non-existent one.

The night of June 5, 1944, Boellner closed the door to his small shop for the last time. The shelves were empty. Everything had been traded or given away. He packed up his engraving tools, and other special items, and put them in his musette bag. The POWS were on a rampage. They were tearing boards off the buildings, making a bonfire. The Japanese guards didn't care. The men were cooking rats and eating them.* It was to be their last night at Davao.

*Interview with Russell Hutchison, 1990.

Transfer North to Manila: June–September 1944

Few of the men slept that night. There was much to do before the 2 A.M. *tenko* (roll call). Russell Hutchison had figured out a way to pack his precious radio and take it with him. West Point class rings, wedding rings, fountain pens, straight razors were patiently sewn inside cuffs and seams to conceal them from a final shakedown by the guards, who had a special fondness for these items. (Later one POW would trade his West Point class ring for a single sip of water.) Canteens were filled, tiny caches of food saved from Red Cross packages were hidden in musette bags.

It was still dark when the men mustered for a last *tenko* at Davao. Rules for good conduct were read by the hated Wada. Each man was issued a towel to use as a blindfold. Their shoes must not be worn but carried. There must be no further escapes. The senior staff officers must give their word that none of their men would attempt an escape.

Each of the 1,239 men was blindfolded, then tied to the man next to him, in groups of from 40 to 60 men, each group bound together by one long continuous rope. If one man fell, they all went down in a tangled mass. Twisted, swearing, trying to remain upright in the packed mass when the trucks would stop and start, being trampled, burned by the ropes, the POWs began their long hellish ride to Lasang dock.

With a two-hour wait in the broiling sun while an old captured American ship renamed the *Yashu Maru* was boarded by Japanese passengers, some of the POWs took precious sips from their canteens. Once aboard, the men could not believe their good fortune when their second Red Cross packages from the January shipment were handed to them. Some of the men had hoped to see some of the Lasang detail, sent to Lasang from Davao some months before, commanded by that exceptional leader of men, a Texan and friend of Boellner's from their Ft. Huachuca days, Captain Rufus H. "Buck" Rogers. Colonel Olson,

88

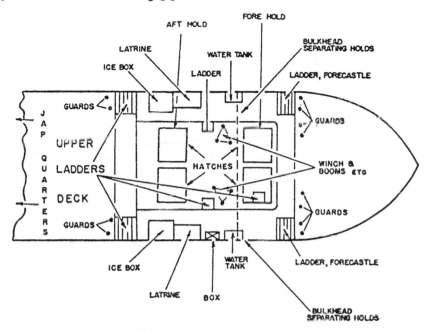

Freighter prison area. Courtesy of Jay Pardue Collection, Monroe, Louisiana, Prisoner of War #1000.

the senior staff officer at Davao, had chosen Rogers to lead 750 men to build a fighter-bomber airstrip for the Japanese, above protests that it violated the rules of the Geneva Convention (which the Japanese preferred to ignore), because in his words, "Rogers was a damn fine leader." He knew he would get the job done, and take care of his men. Those 750 men remained at Lasang until September 1944. They knew the Davao Penal Colony camp was being closed. Russell Hutchison had made certain of that in his messages to "Buck" Rogers.

The *Yashu Maru* sailed with the POWs sitting in each other's laps, crammed below in the stifling cargo hold, for almost a week north to Zamboanga. One American officer, a friend of Boellner's, Colonel John McGee, risked death for freedom when he dived over the ship's rail and swam the distance to the shore. It was territory he knew, where he had been stationed before Pearl Harbor. The next night, a Lt. Wills, bolstered by Colonel McGee's success, escaped the same way. The infuriated Japanese reduced rations en route to Cebu. The POWs were taken ashore there, then loaded onto another smaller ship.

Boellner carried the chassis of the radio in his own musette bag, which he managed to carry from off the *Yashu Maru*. Some of the musette bags and foot lockers belonging to the POWs had not been transferred to the other ship at Cebu, among them the one belonging to a deceased American major whose name was still stenciled on it, the one Russell Hutchison had chosen to put three cans of corned beef in. The heart of the radio was carefully wrapped in kapok inside one of Russell's cans, packed in the major's musette bag, which had been tossed with hundreds of others into the dark hold.

Seeing that these were not being unloaded—the Japanese intended to leave them all in the hold—Russell Hutchison asked permission of one of the guards to retrieve his own musette bag. Oddly, permission was given. It was 140 degrees down in the hold, as the ship had been steeping in the sun for a couple of days. Russell climbed down alone, faced with the dark mountain of abandoned knapsacks and musette bags. He searched until he found it. The corned beef can containing the radio had been opened, and very carefully repacked. The other two full cans of real corned beef were gone.*

The second ship was simply numbered, not named. Hoarded food was gone. The POWs jammed below decks in the dark broiling hold, in a desperate, ugly temper stole from one another. They argued, they fought. MacArthur would invade Mindanao first, they reasoned. Why couldn't they have stayed at Davao camp until he came? This leg of the voyage for many of them was just a taste of what lay ahead. The second ship anchored in Manila on June 26. It had been an exhausting, miserable few days.

Filthy, starved, tired, the POWs were greeted by the Bilibid POWs with a tub full of ice water. There was mail there for some of the Davao POWs. Old acquaintances were renewed. Many of the men had not seen each other since before Pearl Harbor. The Davao POWs felt like "jungle rats being welcomed to a modern hotel."† Grim as the old Bilibid prison was, it was back in civilization. The respite was short-lived. After a few days of processing, Boellner, along with about 700 other officers, was trucked ninety miles north to Cabanatuan.

Cabanatuan was out on the flats. It had been a Philippine Army training camp with makeshift buildings. When it rained it was a bog. When there was no rain it was hot and dusty. Arden's barracks consisted of a dilapidated, long, shuttered building, built to hold 60 men. The Japanese had added a second tier of bunks doubling the capacity of each structure. The POWs had upgraded the camp considerably since those first horrific days in 1942. But food was in very short

*Interview with Russell Hutchison, 1990.
†McCracken, Very Soon Now, Joe.

supply. Anything that could be swallowed was being eaten, bean vines, carrot tops, toads, frogs, snakes, even corn cobs.* One of the Davao POWs asked it there were any iguanas. He had eaten one at Davao. He said it tasted kind of like chicken. He was reassured that iguanas, as well as birds, cats, and dogs were being caught and eaten. So were grub worms and lizards.

At Cabanatuan in 1944 the Japanese were eating very well. They raised a thousand ducks, several hundred chickens, and pigs. Rice was still the staple of their diet, but was supplemented with meat, vegetables, and fruit.†

But the reduced ration of rice for the POWs was of the poorest grade, the floor sweepings mixed with dirt and gravel. Occasionally thre were a few mongo beans, a teaspoonful for each rice cauldron to feed 500 POWs. Whistle weed, a tough fibrous swamp green, was added to the rice gruel for coloring only, as it was indigestible.

The barracks were 50 by 15 feet, built of bamboo and *swali* with roofs of *cogan* grass, set on poles about four feet from the ground. They were open at each end and there were no doors. Inside were ten bays, with upper and lower tiers. The beds were boards running from one wall to the other of each tier. Each bay was intended to house two persons. At peak capacity as many as twelve persons occupied each bay. At different times more than 100 POWs were kept in barracks intended for 40 as the prisoner population increased and decreased.

As the course of the war continued to swing in the Allies' favor, Japanese guards bore down on their "objects of hatred," the POWs, taking a fleeting advantage of superiority over their victims. Beatings, concentrated on the farm detail, were a constant occurrence. Slapping contests where POWs were ordered to face each other, to slap each other fiercely and repeatedly until the guards were satisfied, became an almost daily event, this time involving many of the officers. With the rice ration reduced again and again until only a few spoonfuls were being served at each meal, each grain of rice was carefully counted as it was distributed. The POWs were again losing weight at an alarming rate. Weak and starving, the POWs were forced to cut grass on the Japanese parade grounds with mess kit knives.

*Roy L. Bodine, No Place for Kindness: Prisoner of War Diary [October 1944– September 1945. Privately published.]

†From Report on American POWs Interned by the Japanese in the Philippines, prepared by the Office of the Provost Marshall General, November 19, 1945. National Archives File, regraded unclassified.

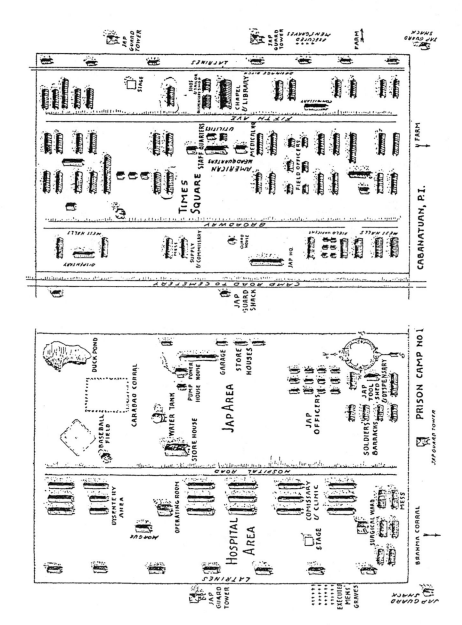

CABANATUAN, P.I.

PRISON CAMP NO 1

In January 1944 work had begun on rebuilding a Japanese airfield about two miles from the camp. From 500 to 1,000 officers and men walked barefoot through the mud, carrying picks and shovels, pushing wheelbarrows to the site. For this heavy manual labor each man was given an ear of corn or *camote* at noon. The work was abandoned in September 1944, when the new camp commander who had come from Davao decided that a detail of carpenters and mechanics, some of the "heartier" men who had worked on the airfield, should build a house for him.*

Boellner and some of the officers in his barracks turned to their tools of trade. One man built a loom from tin cans saved from Red Cross packages. Another made pipes. One fashioned a violin from a tabletop, using only a GI-issue knife for carving.

The days lagged. The men grew weaker. One day a Japanese administrator's assistant came into the barracks carrying a typewriter. Through the interpreter he asked Boellner if he knew how to type. He set the typewriter down on a table and handed him a piece of paper. Boellner was to type the words of an American song for the Japanese commander. Boellner said he did not know the song. Another officer said he knew them, so he hummed and whistled the song, then sang the words while Boellner typed them out. The interpreter looked approvingly at them, gathered up the typewriter and left. The song was "Roll Out the Barrel." It had been a rare diversion.†

By late September 1944 the camp population was reduced to 3,200 men. On September 14, the secret camp radio reported that Palaus and Yap islands had been invaded. The Cabanatuan POWs speculated that MacArthur would invade Mindanao first, then move north to Manila. If they could just hold out a little longer.

About the only redeeming feature of this flat, treeless camp was the naming of the dirt streets and paths in the American section of the camp. "Times Square" was adjacent to the American staff quarters, "Broadway" ran north to south between the Japanese and American section fences. "Fifth Avenue" separated the POWs' barracks from their chapel, library, and commissary. This touch of home helped many a man preserve his sanity in this far-off hell.§

Opposite: **Layout of Prison Camp 1, Cabanatuan. (Courtesy of Jay Pardue Collection, Monroe, Louisiana, Prisoner of War #1000.)**

*Ibid.   † *Comments of Colonel Cain, 1944–45.*
§Report on American POWs Interned by the Japanese in the Philippines.

Bilibid Prison
and Aboard the *Oryoku Maru*:
October–December 1944

By mid–October one of the many rumors proved to be true. The camp was being uprooted. Only 511 of the very sick and disabled POWS would remain at Cabanatuan. The rest were being transported back to old Bilibid prison in Manila.

Some five or six days before October 19 when the POWS were scheduled to leave, as they were going about their dreary daily routines, they raised their heads to the sky to the unfamiliar roar that was coming closer and closer. A man pointed. *There they were!* Formations of American planes with fighter escorts flying at high altitude, winging north to Luzon. Their sound was distinctive — big, new powerful planes with four engines, not two. These were the superfortresses — new air warfare planes.

Wonder-struck, overcome, and stunned, some men merely stared with tears streaming down their haggard faces. Others yelled and whooped. They clapped each other on the back and danced jigs. "Didn't I tell you?" One man slumped to his knees, hands clasped in prayer. "You lazy slackers — where you been?" "Son of a beautiful bitch — keep coming — Mac — Keep right on comin' — ." They had made it.

Inspection was at 7 A.M. The POWS were allowed to carry only two cans of food with them to Bilibid. Roy Bodine put a little sugar and peanuts in a sock.* Six small trucks carried forty men each, most of them standing. Another inspection, then they were given a piece of cornbread and a handful of dry rice. At 11 A.M. another big formation of American planes flew over. The trucks kept moving. Hot and weary, they arrived at Bilibid at 4 P.M.

Bodine, No Place for Kindness.

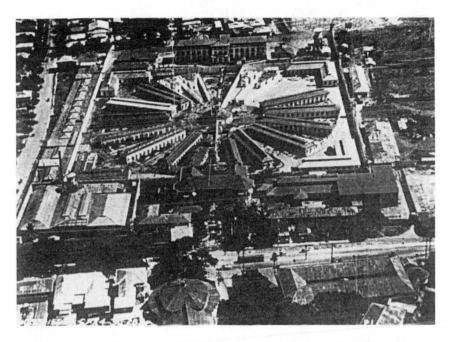

Bilibid Prison, Manila, Philippine Islands, aerial view 1941–44. (Courtesy of Walt Regehr Collection.)

Bilibid was again swelled to capacity with 2,000 men. The POWs there were very excited about recent bombings. MacArthur was getting very close. The Japanese were panic ridden. The ration was two meals a day, all *lugao*, less than a canteen cup—the worst ration yet. The new groups went around to see friends, some hardly recognizable at 97 pounds, most very sick with beriberi and dysentery.

There was another air raid on October 25, 50 planes with fighters. Colonel Beecher and staff arrived from Cabanatuan, with the great news that MacArthur had landed on Leyte on October 20.

"We hope the Japs can't get us out of here," wrote one prisoner, Dr. Roy L. Bodine, whose diary would later be published.* But it certainly appeared that was what they intended. Rosters were being made up, woolen uniforms were being brought to the POWs. The men were divided into three groups and were told they would leave on Friday. "Hopes go up and down," Bodine wrote. "Rice getting thinner, smaller each day. Men are very weak."

On November 2, the men were called over to get foot lockers.

Ibid.

Morale went down too. They were given Japanese trousers and jackets, which were very small. It was both funny and sad. Major Bob Nelson sold his Eastman for 900 pesos, and bought mongo beans, a short kilo, one and a half cups.*

"More bombings on November 5th and 6th. Everyone is out of tobacco. We hear we have won a big Naval battle between Saipan and Formosa. Mac is coming slowly, don't expect him for awhile, probably on Luzon about the first half of December. Hope he makes it for Christmas, and we are still here," Bodine wrote.

The days of November dragged on. The Manila port area was bombed. The men could see big fires raging in the distance. Beans and sugar, when they could get them, went from $15 to $23 per kilo, or could be traded for watches and rings. On the fifteenth there was a big flash and explosion which shook the prison buildings. Japanese were shooting at the buildings across the street. A firefight between the Filipinos and Japanese was everyone's guess. It sounded like real war again.

The 900-calorie-a-day diet left the men very weak, with little strength to even move about the prison confines. They were getting used to hearing explosions and shooting. Bodine managed to scrounge some banana skins to boil to make coffee.

For Thanksgiving, November 30, the mess tried to make do with one and a half sacks of beans and a half cup of thin soup for 2,000 men. They made a pudding of rice and *camotes* with ginger and a little sugar. "The worst Thanksgiving of my life," wrote Bodine.

December 6, 1944, came with no bombings for 11 days, Bodine recorded in his diary. "They're bombing northern Luzon every day. Everyone is collecting recipes, making menus, listing the names of eating places in the States. Classes are still being held, languages and crafts, mostly.

"December 7th, 1944, and today is the end of the third year of war. Japs didn't celebrate like they did three years ago. Barrage balloons are up. Waiting.

"December 11th, and no bombing in Manila for 16 days. Typhoons have slowed Mac. Can only hope and pray." December 12 and the Japanese ordered examination of patients to see what number can be moved. Soap and toilet paper were issued.

December 12, 1944, "It was announced tonight at 6:30 P.M. *tenko* (roll call) that our detail would leave for Japan at 8 A.M. Reveille at

Ibid.

4 A.M. Six officers are to share one foot locker. We tried to eat as much as we could, and set out beans to soak. We'll try to have them cooked on the electric plate, but have to wait our turn. We packed what food we had saved. We tried to take all clothing, soap, anything of value at all. We wrote letters and left them with Bilibid POW friends. Went to bed at 2 A.M. Up at 4 A.M."

The men formed ranks at 7·30 A.M. Two more hours were spent checking rosters and counting the men, comprised of 1,035 officers, 500 enlisted men, 37 British soldiers, and 47 civilians. Some of the men were in terrible shape, mere walking skeletons. At the sound of five gongs, at almost high noon, after more delays, the men were reassembled.*

Boellner shouldered his pack with the best of them. The walls of old Bilibid prison cast rounded shadows across the men. Some staggered to remain upright in the noontide heat. They formed ranks of four abreast in the usual Japanese groups of 100. The POWs remaining at Bilibid gathered for a last salute.

"For God's sake, tell the American people the truth," a fellow POW told Boellner in parting.† Boellner nodded his promise.

"Whatever happens, we have the satisfaction of knowing we're beating the pants off them now —" another POW cheered.

The order to march was shouted. Filing out, the column of POWs jerked thumbs up in confidence, or made the V sign, or crossed fingers for good luck. Men whose hearts were breaking showed their fellow Americans a smile. These tired heroes of Bataan, Corregidor, and the Visayas, may have been starved, ragged, but never had they been so truly magnificent, so deeply worthy of the humble respect and admiration of every American.§

"Come '45 — we're all alive," the words echoed to silence behind the POWs filing out.

The three-block-long column, thin from three years of confinement, guarded by Japanese with bayonets, shuffled forth under a broiling sun into the dusty streets of Manila. Red Cross shoes, badly worn and mud-caked from the airfield work up at Cabanatuan, hung from around the necks of some of the POWs. Some were lucky enough to wear trousers. Some wore only G-strings. Some had found old civilian suits. A few had hats.

People lined the streets of Manila to stare. Many of the loyal

---

*Ibid.   †McCracken, Very Soon Now, Joe.   §Ibid.

Filipinos gave the V sign in secret. One stooped, wrinkled Filipino woman put her fingers crossed to her mouth, giving her sign of loyalty. In the lace-curtained parlors of the poor Philippine homes, the radios were turned on full blast as the column of POWs approached, then turned down to silence after the column passed, in an indirect salute from the underground.

Bicycles, pushcarts, *caratelas*, carts with auto wheels pulled by man or beast, and a fair sprinkling of Japanese in cars dotted the streets. The column moved down Quezon Avenue and around the Walled City. There were soldiers everywhere. Lawns once beautiful stood in weeds; the pavement was broken and filthy. The street cars were no longer in use. General Luna Street was fenced off with a sentry.

As the column moved to the "Million-Dollar Pier," Pier 7, they saw firsthand the results of Allied bombings. Bachrach Motors had been destroyed. The big buildings of the Army and Navy Club, the big hotels were intact. The bay was full of hulks. The pier looked wrecked, but was in use.

Tied up at Pier 7 was a junk and two big ships. The POW column reached there at about 2 P.M. The pier was crowded with Japanese civilians by the hundreds, all well-dressed, with wives, babies, luggage, and often with large casks of sugar.

One of the large ships was the *Oryoku Maru*, a passenger ship from the Tokyo-South American run before the war, 9,500 tons, built in Nagasaki in 1939. The ship had been elegant once, but now showed wear. It was camouflaged in a dull gray paint. There to greet the POWs were several Japanese whom the men already knew. There was General Koa, in charge of all the POWs in the Philippines. There was Lt. N. Nogi, director of the Bilibid hospital, a former Seattle physician, who, in most cases, had been kind to the Americans. The ship was not marked. The Japanese women and children were put on the lower deck. The loading of the civilians took until almost 5 P.M.

The Japanese decided to fill the aft hold first, and to put aboard the 700 highest ranking officers before the others. Boellner was in this group. The aft hold's hatch was cut off from free circulation of air by bulkheads fore and aft. A long slanting wooden staircase dipped 35 feet through the hatch, down which the POWs crept.

When the first officers reached the bottom of the ladder they were

Opposite: The December ship, the *Oryoku Maru*. (Courtesy of the Steamship Historical Society Collection, University of Baltimore Library.)

met by Sergeant Dau, well known at Davao Penal Colony. His men used brooms to beat the American officers back as far as possible into the dim bays of the hold.

Long before the hold was filled the air was foul, and breathing was difficult. But the Japanese kept driving more men down the ladder from the deck, and Dau and his men kept squeezing the first-comers farther back into the airless dark.

The first officers who had descended were sitting in bays, a double-tier system of wooden stalls. The lower bays were three feet high. A man could neither stand, nor extend his legs. Each bay was about nine feet from passageway to rear wall. The Japanese guards insisted that the POWS could sit in rows four feet deep, each man's back against his neighbor's knee, in this nine-foot depth.

When the Japanese on deck looked down through the hatch, they saw a pit of living men, staring upward, their chests and shoulders heaving as they struggled for air and wriggled for a little more space. The first fights began when men started passing out. Only the front men in each bay were getting enough air.

The forward hold was loaded next, with 600 men. In this hold there were no ventilators or portholes. It was as bad as the aft hold crowding with a wooden shelf four feet off the floor. The midship hold was loaded last with 319 men, mostly Army and Navy medics and civilians.

At about 5 P.M. the *Oryoku Maru* started its engines and moved smoothly with little vibration, out into the bay to the breakwater where it stopped. Down in the fetid, airless three holds, in closing darkness the POWS realized into whose hands their fate had been given. The guards were mixed, but mostly they were Formosans, or Taiwanese, as they liked to be called. They were commanded by Lt. Junsaburo Toshino, an officer of somewhat Western and Prussian appearance, with short clipped hair, spectacles, and a rough manner. He, in turn had relegated the command to the interpreter, Shunusuke Wada, the hunchbacked tyrant known to all the POWS.

At the breakwater the *Oryoku Maru* became a part of the convoy of five merchant ships, guarded by a cruiser and several destroyers and lighter craft. They moved without lights. Hoarse shouts from the hold of the *Oryoku Maru* could be heard across the water. As the air in the holds grew scarcer, the pleas for air grew louder and more raucous. Before long, the Japanese threatened to board bown the hatches and cut off all the air.

In the fast darkness, the Japanese lowered down into the writhing hold eight wooden buckets filled with fried rice, cabbage and fried seaweed. Amid screams and wild shouts, the buckets were handed around. The officers who had mess kits scooped in the buckets, the others simply grabbed blindly with their hands. Most ate, but those in the rear bays got little.

Shunusuke Wada, the interpreter, was annoyed. He stood with hands on hips, glaring into the hold, protected by his Formosan guards.

"You are disturbing the Japanese women and children," he called down from the top of the hatch to Commander Frank Bridget who was trying to maintain some kind of order among the suffocating men. "Stop your noise or the hatches will be closed."

The noise of crazed men could not be stopped. The hatches were closed. At about 10 P.M. some of the men crept up the ladder and parted the planks slightly so some air could get through.

Wada came again to the edge of the writhing pit. "Unless you are quiet, I shall give the order to fire down into the hold." There was a space of quiet, an exhausted quiet.

The seaweed, cabbage, and rice mixed with fish made the men desperately thirsty. The four-gallon buckets of water and one four-gallon bucket of tea lowered much earlier had all been drunk. Some of the POWs drank from their canteens. In the stifling heat of temperatures well above 100 degrees the men began to sweat. By midnight most had stripped down to their G-strings. Men ill with dysentary and diarrhea pleaded to be allowed the use of latrines. The Formosans passed down a five-gallon bucket. These soon overflowed.

Men began to suffocate. Chaplains tried to soothe the thirsty sweltering masses with soft prayers. The order, "At Ease!" was ignored as men slipped into unconsciousness, only to awaken screaming.

Around midnight, one began calling, "Lieutenant Toshino — Lieutenant Toshino!" Others insane with thirst and suffocating shouted, "Knife that man!" There would be a scream, a struggle. "Get Denny — he did it — grab him!" then another struggle. The milling and shoving in the pitch blackness, the horrific stench of overspilling human waste, brought new hysteria and madness. Some chose the short way home. Death took soldiers old and new. One officer had been a middle-weight boxing champion at Annapolis. Some were part of Shanghai's famous 4th Marines. Some ran for the ladder to the deck and collapsed. They lay where they died, for in the darkness only the man next to him knew a comrade-in-arms had died. In the 130-degree heat it took a long time for a body to cool.

In the aft hold where Boellner was, 30 men died of suffocation the first night.

Two hours past midnight, the *Oryoku Maru* in convoy moved beyond the breakwater and out to sea. A little fresh air seeped down into the battened holds. At first light the POWs looked about them. Some men were in a stupor, some were dead, a few were insane. In the aft hold there were two decks and a bottom hatch leading into the bilge. The most violent of the insane were lowered into the subhold.

The suffered breathing of hundreds of lungs made huge drops of moisture that clung to the bulkheads. Men scraped off the moisture and drank it. Naked, sitting like galley slaves between each other's legs, they looked at their hands. Fingers seemed long and unusually thin. The ends were white, wrinkled, as though they had been soaked in hot water for hours. Their throats were sandpaper-dry. Already they were in the weakening stages of severe dehydration.

Dawn on December 14, 1944, brought United States Navy planes from the carrier *Hornet* to the skies in search of enemy prey. On patrol from a raid off the east coast of Luzon, twelve fighter planes sighted the convoy passing Corregidor and heading north.

The POWs down in the holds heard the cry, "Air raid!" just as buckets of rice and fish were being lowered. Japanese gun crews leaped to their places. At 8 A.M. the Navy planes dived on the convoy with bombs, rockets, and machine guns. No bombs connected, but smoke was noted from the stern of the transport. The Japanese returned fire with .50-caliber three-inch, and pom-poms.

In the holds below, helpless men huddled against one another, or lay flat or against bulwarks for protection. The airless holds now filled with suffocating dust and smoke. There were some wounded from splinters off the bridge and fragments from the strafing that came down the hatch. Entombed men prayed. There was a lull, then it all began again with a new attack wave two hours later. The second wave left, but returned for another attack. One three-inch antiaircraft gun on the forward deck of the ship had been damaged, but machine guns and pom-poms kept up a steady fire. Japanese escort ships turned to open sea to escape.

Commander Frank Bridget sat at the top of the ladder in his hold, like an announcer in the press box, he would call the plays. "I can see two planes going for a freighter off our starboard side — now two more are detached from the formation. I think they may be coming for us. They are! Everybody duck!" Bullets rattled on the deck plates like hail.

Near noontime the POWs took careful sips of precious water

lowered during an earlier lull, three-fourths of a cup of water for twenty men. In the sweltering semi-darkness the men waited for the next attack. Some prayed the ship would be hit and end their agony. Late afternoon the planes returned for their heaviest of nine attacks of the day. There were three hits near the bridge and the stern. They could hear a crackling of flames, and fire hoses being used. During the lulls the men had become numbed, drowsy in the close heat. Panic and excitement of the earlier attacks had worn off. Some even slept. All were terribly thirsty.

Near dusk, the stunned POWs revived a little. The attacks were over for the day. They were still alive. From the upper decks they could hear sounds of screaming, of children crying. Blood seeped down through torn decks splattering over them. They Navy pilots had brought death and terror, but to the POWs they brought light and air. The *Oryoku Maru* weighed anchor, turning east, then south, then west again, then north, edging back to shore.

The 2,000 Japanese passengers had suffered, too. From the forward hold, the interpreter Wada called up American doctors to treat the wounded. Lt. Colonel William North and Lt. Colonel Jack W. Schwartz, along with several other doctors and corpsmen climbed out of the hold into the fresh air and twilight to offer help. The carnage above decks was appalling. The American detail pleaded, then demanded that the POWs be given water. Wada refused. The American doctors and corpsmen worked for hours. They were given a drink of water and returned to the hold.

The *Oryoku Maru* with a damaged rudder had run aground off Olongapo Point on the island of Luzon. In its cargo holds were hundreds of POWs who had spent more than twenty-four hours there. Many had died of suffocation, and heat, some at the hands of men driven insane. They all were hungry, thirsty, fouled by their own filth. For the next few hours while the captain of the *Oryoku Maru* attempted to free the ship, discipline in the holds again began to crack. At about 8 P.M. the ship floated free and moved in toward the American Naval base at Olongapo.

Near 10 P.M. the Japanese passengers began leaving the ship. Japanese guards, fearing an all-scale riot from POWs trying to escape the holds, stood with machine guns ready. The POW officers in charge of each hold knew it would be mass slaughter if the POWs reached the decks. They posted guards at the foot of the ladder.

Sixteen chaplains were distributed between the three holds. Most of them had their Bibles or breviaries. Some read aloud to the men to quiet them. The milling started again. Naked men staggering in the darkness, out of their minds, searching for water. A Navy chaplain took out his prayer book again. Suddenly he stopped reading and began tearing out the pages. He made a dash for the ladder. One of the American guards pulled him down before the Formosan could fire. They tied the chaplain to the ladder until he quieted down.

Commander Frank Bridget, his voice hoarse from continuous shouting, never left his press box. He was relieved occasionally by an officer of the 4th Marines, Andrew J. Mathiesen. Mathiesen had a steady cool smile. In the fetid darkness the POWS could still see that smile.

"Not going to Japan, boys," he would say. "Still right off old Subic Bay. Not going to Japan."

Men crazed with thirst and despair imagined they heard men plotting against them in the blackness. One of them approached the chief warrant officer.

"Look," he said. "I've lost my nerve. The fellows over there in the bay with me are going to kill me. I showed them my canteen was empty, but they don't believe me." The officers told him to calm down, he was imagining things. In an hour the man was back. This time he was ordered back to his bay. The next morning he was found dead, knifed.

Some of the men thought they were back home. They talked to their loved ones, fought with their neighbors. Others thought they were still back at the camps, Bilibid, Davao, or Cabanatuan. One thought he was planting rice, raving about how cool the mud felt.

After the *Oryoku Maru* had dropped anchor, no air came down the hatches. Animals could not have been shipped under such conditions and survived. The closeness, the blackness brought on crowd poisoning and its symptoms: the body broke out in excessive sweat, causing a swoon, or it turned to cold sweat with dizziness and vomiting. Wandering men bumped into each other. Some were swinging canteens. Many were mistaken for an attacker and killed. Others let themselves go completely, and like animals bit the men nearest them. Amid the screams, the moaning, the unintelligible ravings, the American doctors began calling for quiet. It was a nightmare gone mad.

In the last hours of darkness of the second horrible night, the Japanese sent word to Commander Portz, the American commander, and the commander of each hold that the POWS were going to be allowed to leave the ship.

Commander Bridget in the aft hold made the announcement from his press box.

"Good news, boys. We're going to be put ashore here. The Japanese civilians have all been put ashore, and our turn is next." The POWs were told they could take their pants and shirts, mess kits and canteens. They could not take their musette bags or their shoes.

It began to get light, but there was no pier in sight. The Japanese passengers had evidently been taken ashore in launches. The POWs gathered up what they were told they could take. Wada shouted down the hold that the first 25 men were to get ready to come up the ladder.

It was 8 A.M. on a clear Sunday morning. The date was December 15, 1944, ten days before Christmas. The first 25 men climbed up, past Formosan guns, and out of the hold. The guards signaled that the POWs were to be used as oarsmen to ferry them to shore. The first boat was loaded quickly. Chief Boatswain Clarence Taylor took six men and himself into the first boat. The eight others were Japanese soldiers.

The second group of 25 POWs had started up the ladder. The Japanese guards began shouting, "Air raid!" He motioned the men to go back down into the hold saying, "Many planes! Many planes!" Lieutenant Toshino, the Japanese commander in charge of the POWs signaled Taylor's boat to shove off from the rail.

The first wave of the *Hornet*'s planes, a dozen fighter bombers in four flights of three each, began their dives. The first bombs were small ones. The *Oryoku Maru* seemed the only target. The ship took a hit. A couple of small holes were blown in the side of the midship hold. Waves lapped in from near misses. There was another hit forward and water was running in. The death ship began to list.

The next assault planes carried 500-pound bombs. On the first dive the Navy pilots watched two bombs miss. Their rockets hit, and their strafing was on target. Boellner crowded at the foot of the ladder with his brother officers. He carried his musette bag with Chaplain Ted Howden's Episcopal vestments and prayer book. He had made a promise to the chaplain from New Mexico, who had died a year before, to take them home. He listened during a bombing lull while a Japanese sentry shrieked, "Speedo! All go home!"

The lull lasted only moments. One heavy bomb striking barely aft of the hatch rained splinters into the hold full of naked men. The iron girder supporting the hatch planks blew into the hold, felling the men waiting. Those still standing made a wild rush for the ladder. The deck above was perforated with holes. Light streamed through. But then yellowish haze began to appear in the bays.

"Fire!" "Let me out!" "I'd rather be shot than burn!" one of the men yelled.

The ladder was splintered and sagging. Men who began to climb were bleeding from the nose and mouth from concussion. One officer from New Mexico made the top of the ladder only to be shot three times by a sentry. There was no stopping the men now. The Japanese sentries fled to the other side of the ship. Those POWs who reached the deck were met with a terrible silence.

The guns were unmanned. The planes had flown away.

Arden Boellner's story ended in those last moments during the short infamous voyage of the *Oryoku Maru*. For others who survived, new ordeals were just beginning.

Of the 1,619 American officers, enlisted men, British soldiers, and civilians who set foot aboard the *Oryoku Maru* on December 13, 1944, fewer than 300 would live to be liberated.

Appendix: Letters

GENERAL HEADQUARTERS
UNITED STATES ARMY FORCES, PACIFIC
OFFICE OF THE COMMANDER-IN-CHIEF

APO 500
25 October 1945

Dear Mrs. Boellner:

My deepest sympathy goes to you
in the death of your husband, Lieutenant Colonel Arden
R. Boellner, who died in action against the enemy.

You may have some consolation
in the memory that he, along with his comrades-in-arms
who died on Bataan and Corregidor and in prison camps,
gave his life for his country. It was largely their
magnificent courage and sacrifices which stopped the
enemy in the Philippines and gave us the time to arm
ourselves for our return to the Philippines and the
final defeat of Japan. Their names will be enshrined
in our country's glory forever.

In your husband's death I have
lost a gallant comrade and mourn with you.

Very faithfully,

Douglas MacArthur

Mrs. Arden R. Boellner
508 N Missouri Avenue
Roswell, New Mexico

WAR DEPARTMENT

WASHINGTON
Room 4-C-261
Pentagon Bldg.

21 December 1945

Mrs. Arder R. Boellner
508 N. Missouri Ave.,
Roswell, New Mexico

My dear Mrs. Boellner:

Your husband was a member of my Command when I served
as Commanding General of the Visayan-Mindanao Force in defense
of the Philippines.

I last saw your husband in September of 1942 in the
Japanese Prison Camp in Mindanao, at which time I was taken
north to Formosa and later to Manchuria by the Japanese. I
lost all contact with him and other officers in that camp
until May of 1945 when I met some of them in Mukden, Manchuria.
These officers were the survivors of the ill-fated Japanese
Prison Ship that sailed north from Manila to Japan in December
1944. They told me of the death of your husband together with
many other officers on that ship.

Your husband was a fine, loyal officer who did excellent
work while serving with my Command. He was always cheerful
and willing; he made a lasting impression on all with whom he
came in contact.

I deeply regret his loss and mourn with you his passing.
Mrs. Sharp joins me in extending to you our heartfelt sympathy
in your bereavement.

Sincerely,

W. J. Sharp

WILLIAM F. SHARP
Major General
U. S. Army

August 9, 1945.

My dear Mrs. Boellner:

You will shortly receive the Purple Heart medal, which has been posthumously awarded by direction of the President to your husband, Lieutenant Colonel Arden R. Boellner, Infantry. It is sent as a tangible expression of the country's gratitude for his gallantry and devotion.

It is sent to you, as well, with my deepest personal sympathy for your bereavement. The loss of a loved one is beyond man's repairing, and the medal is of slight value; not so, however, the message it carries. We are all comrades in arms in this battle for our country, and those who have gone are not, and never will be, forgotten by those of us who remain. I hope you will accept the medal in evidence of such remembrance.

Sincerely yours,

Henry L Stimson

Mrs. Arden R. Boellner,
     508 North Missouri Avenue,
          Roswell, New Mexico.

THE CHIEF OF STAFF
WAR DEPARTME. T
WASHINGTON. D. C.

OFFICIAL BUSINESS

PENALTY FOR PRIVATE USE TO AVOID
PAYMENT OF POSTAGE. $300

Mrs. Arden R. Boellner
508 North Missouri Avenue
Roswell, New Mexico

---

*General Marshall
extends his deep sympathy
in your bereavement. Your husband
fought valiantly in a supreme hour
of his country's need. His memory will
live in the grateful heart of our nation*

2627 Oakdale
Houston, Texas
Jan. 1, 1944

Judge James B. McGhee
Roswell, New Mexico

Dear Judge McGhee:

Having known Lieut. Col. Boellner well during our months of internment together at Davao, Mindanao, I am grateful to relay my news of him to his family and friends.

Colonel Boellner was given a job as the camp craftsman, repairing watches for the camp. He was highly respected by the Japanese for his ability to keep our timepieces going.

Having that administrative job, Colonel Boellner was exempted from the heavy manual labor assigned some of the prisoners. When I last saw him, in February of this year, he was in good physical shape, relatively excellent in comparison. I never knew him to be ill.

He never lost his ready humor, and his good spirits. Colonel Boellner used to get lots of laughs about his being awakened by fellow barracks-men because of his snoring. We teased him a good bit about that snoring which he attributed to his easy conscience.

I recall that Colonel Boellner once gave me quite a lengthy and intricate lesson on watch-repairing. One of these days, when I get time, I intend to try to utilize his teachings.

He was among a group of the 1200 remaining prisoners at Davao, whom the Japanese transported north, presumably to Japan, in July of this year. We were told that their convoy arrived safely at its destination. Indications are that they were sent to Japanese camps near Osaka and other cities.

A group of 750 men who were later on the Jap ship torpedoed off the Philippines (from which 82 of us escaped) had been transferred away from Davao in Feb. of this year. We were taken to Lasang to work on an airfield.

One of the officers in our troop of escapees may be able to give you even more recent information about Colonel Boellner. He is Col. John H. McGee, of Minot, North Dakota. Colonel McGee remained at Davao until June of this year.

Please give my kindest regards to Mrs. Boellner and Family.

You might assure her that a fine medical treatment developed

by our Army medical corps for returning prisoners of war, will
have Colonel Boellner on his feet in a matter of days. Our main
ailment was lack of beefsteaks.

Sharing your hope that 1945 will be a victorious year, in which
all our Japanese-held Americans will be released, I am

Faithfully yours,

Morris L. Shoss,
Major CAC.

*Author's note: Colonel Morris Shoss was one of the 87 survivors
of another hellship, the *Shinyo Maru,* a prison transport carrying the
Lasang Detail of 750 American prisoners of war, commanded by Lt.
Colonel Bill Rogers, from Davao north to Manila. The unmarked
Shinyo Maru was torpedoed by a U.S. Navy submarine on September 7, 1944, and sunk.

Guest House, Walter Reed
General Hospital
Washington, D.C.
4 January, 1946

Dear Mrs. Boellner,

In writing this letter I earnestly hope I shall not renew your
grief over the loss of your husband, Colonel Boellner. If I do,
please forgive me for my only desire is to let you know that Arden
was a splendid soldier and his failure to come through our ordeal
has caused me much sorrow.

Arden and I served together from the latter part of March
1942, up to the date we were ordered to surrender, May 10, 1942.
He was executive of the command I had during that period. It
consisted of several regiments of infantry, a battalion of Philippine
Scouts, a detachment of 295 mountain howitzers, and several other
detachments. His duties were of great importance as his position
was a key one and was most arduous. He discharged them in a
truly fine manner.

After the surrender he and I were imprisoned with the other
American officers on Mindanao at Camp Casisang, Mindanao.
There he and I lived together until September 6, 1942, when I was

shipped with other general officers and colonels to Formosa by way of Manila. I did not see him after that date. I, with the others mentioned, was kept on Formosa until October 1944, then shipped to Manchuria where we remained until August 19th when we were released by the Russians.

My contacts with Arden are the brightest spots of my experiences in the Philippines after the outbreak of war. He gave much of his time and skill helping his comrades in prison. His kindness to all won him many friends.

Shortly before I was transferred from Camp Casisang he, Colonel Wade Killen, and I, had several pictures taken using Arden's camera. The snapshots were very small but rather good nevertheless. Being small they were easily concealed, thus I was able to successfully hide them when searched by our captors from time to time — and finally to bring them home with me. Since the pictures are possibly the last Arden had taken of himself I felt I should have them enlarged, and a copy of each enlargement, two in all sent to you. I received the enlargements yesterday and am mailing them to you by ordinary mail, registered. I would have enclosed them with this letter had it not seemed advisable to let you know beforehand that they are on the way. No doubt you have much better pictures of Arden, still it seemed to me you would want those being sent.

Arden often spoke of you and the rest of his family. When we parted he gave me his business card with your name written on it — Hazel — as I recall. Our agreement was that if but one survived, the survivor would communicate with the other's family. I succeeded in keeping the card until a few weeks ago when I misplaced it, and have so far been unable to find it. Had I not misplaced it I would have enclosed it with this letter.

In explanation, Mrs. Boellner, of my delay in writing you — I was flown back to the U.S. on Sept. 15th as a hospital patient and have been in the hospital ever since. Only recently have I been permitted to do any writing. My health is now much better than it was, but will not permit me to return to active duty and so I expect to be retired in the near future.

Mrs. Dalton joins me in sending you our best wishes.

Most sincerely yours

W. F. Dalton
Col. Inf. U.S.A.

Bibliography

Beloti, James H. and William M., *Corregidor, Saga of a Fortress*. New York: Harper and Row, 1967.

Bodine, Roy L., *No Place for Kindness: Prisoner of War Diary, October 1944–September 1945*. Privately published.

Boellner family collection, 1941–47.

Boyle, Martin, *Yanks Don't Cry*. New York: Random House, 1963.

Breur, William B., *Retaking the Philippines*. New York: St. Martin's, 1986.

Brown, Charles M., Lt. Col. AUS Ret., *The Oryoku Maru Story*. Privately published, August 1983.

Devereaux, James P. S., *The Story of Wake Island*. New York: J. B. Lippincott, 1947.

Dyess, William E., *The Dyess Story*. New York: C. P. Putnam's Sons, 1944.

Falk, Stanley A., *Bataan: The March of Death*. New York: W. W. Norton, 1962.

Frankel, Stanley A., *Unit Histories: 37th Division in World War II*. Washington, D.C.: Infantry Journal, 1948.

Kerr, E. Barlett, *Surrender and Survival: The Experience of American POWs in the Pacific 1941–1945*. New York: William Morrow, 1985.

Knox, Donald, *Death March*. New York: Harcourt Brace Jovanovich, 1981.

McCracken, Alan, *Very Soon Now, Joe*. New York: Hobson, 1947.

McGee, John H., *Rice and Salt*. San Antonio, Texas: Naylor, 1962.

Mellnik, S. M., *Philippine Diary*. New York: Van Nostrand, Reinhold, 1969.

Morton, Louis, *The Fall of the Philippines: U.S. Army in World War II*. Washington, D.C.: Government Printing Office, 1953.

National Archives, Historical Manuscript File, *United States Army Forces in the Philippines, Report of Operations of USAFFE and USFIP in the Philippine Islands 1941–1942*, Washington, D.C.: Microfilm publication, Department of the Army, 1971.

National Archives, holdings, *Prisoner of War Information Bureau, Office of the Provost Marshal General*. Not for Publication. Received May 7, 1943, Allies Division Information Branch, Cable Process Record, Microfilm publication.

National Archives, *Report on American Prisoners of War Interned by the Japanese in the Philippines*, Prepared by the Office of the Provost Marshal General, November 19, 1945, Secret/Confidential/Restricted Regraded, Order Secretary of the Army.

Stewart, Sidney, *Give Us This Day*. New York: W. W. Norton, 1957.
Toland, John, *But Not in Shame*. New York: Random House, 1961.
_____, *The Rising Sun: The Decline and Fall of the Japanese Empire, 1936–1945*.
    New York: Random House, 1970.
Wainwright, Johnathan, *General Wainwright's Story*. Edited by Bob Considine,
    Garden City, New York: Doubleday, 1946.

Index

117